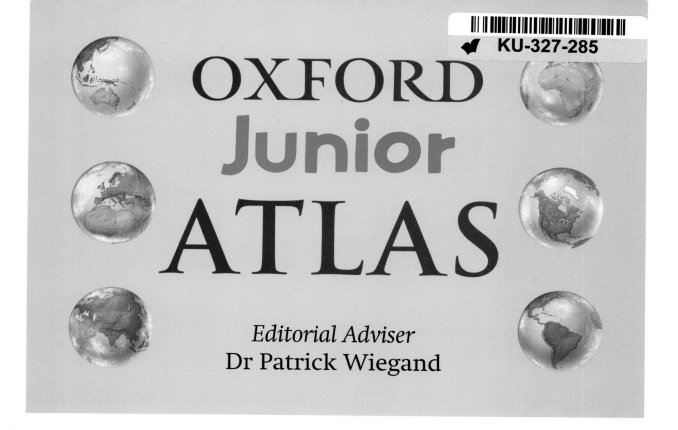

OXFORD Junior ATLAS

Editorial Adviser
Dr Patrick Wiegand

OXFORD
UNIVERSITY PRESS

Great Clarendon Street, Oxford OX2 6DP

Oxford University Press is a department of the University of Oxford.
It furthers the University's objective of excellence in research, scholarship,
and education by publishing worldwide in

Oxford   New York

Auckland   Cape Town   Dar es Salaam   Hong Kong   Karachi
Kuala Lumpur   Madrid   Melbourne   Mexico City   Nairobi
New Delhi   Shanghai   Taipei   Toronto

With offices in

Argentina   Austria   Brazil   Chile   Czech Republic   France   Greece
Guatemala   Hungary   Italy   Japan   Poland   Portugal   Singapore
South Korea   Switzerland   Thailand   Turkey   Ukraine   Vietnam

Oxford is a registered trade mark of Oxford University Press
in the UK and in certain other countries

ISBN 0 19 832158 9 (hardback)

ISBN 0 19 832157 0 (paperback)

1 3 5 7 9 10 8 6 4 2

Printed in Singapore

Acknowledgements

**The publishers would like to thank the following for permission to
reproduce the following photographs:**

Bryan & Cherry Alexander Photography: 58 middle, 61 middle; Austin
Brown/Aviation Picture Library: 66 right; British Petroleum Shipping Ltd
(Fotoflite): 67 right; Comstock Photo Library: 54, 58 bottom left, 59 middle,
60 bottom middle, 61 right; The Environmental Picture Library: 63 left; Greg
Evans International: 58 bottom middle, 58 bottom right, 59 bottom left; FLPA:
60 bottom right; Robert Harding Picture Library Ltd: 33 top, 37 top right, 37
bottom left, 60 top right, 62 top; Jason Hawkes Aerial Photo Library: 7 top
left, 7 top right, 7 middle; Holt Studios International: 31 all; The Hutchison
Library: 33 bottom, 62 bottom; David Keith Jones/Images of Africa Photobank:
59 bottom right; Mark Mason: 4 top right, 5; National Remote Sensing Centre
(Airphotogroup): 4 top left; Marilyn O'Brien: 37 bottom right; Christine Osborne
Pictures: 60 bottom left; Port of Felixstowe: 67 left; The Photolibrary Wales:
7 bottom left, 7 bottom right, 33 middle, 37 top left; Rex Features: 62 middle;

Science Photo Library: 14, 56 middle, 57, 60 top left, 66 left; Sealand Aerial
Photography: 13, 30 all, 32 all, 34 left; Skyscan: 34 right; Still Pictures: 36, 56
bottom; The Telegraph Colour Library: 59 bottom middle, 60 top middle, 65;
Tropix Photographic Library: 63 right; United States Atlantic Fleet Submarine
Force: Public Affairs Office 55.

Cover image: Tom Van Sant / Geosphere Projection, Santa Monica, Science
Photo Library.

The illustrations are by Chapman Bounford, Hardlines, Mike Harkins, and
Gary Hinks.

The page design is by Adrian Smith.

2 Contents

Atlas information

The British Isles

The United Kingdom

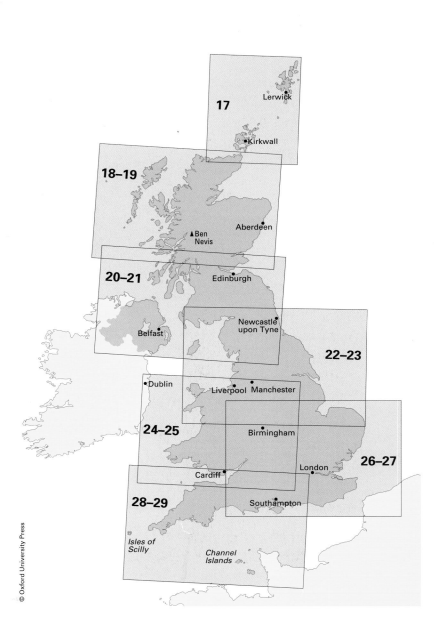

This book is to

This book is to

Contents

Continents and Poles

The World

Liskeard **28** C3
Lismore *island* **18** D1
Lithuania 38 D2
Littlehampton **29** G3
Little Minch *sound* **18** C2
Little Ouse *river* **27** E3

Index

4 Round Earth

A globe shows the Earth as a sphere.

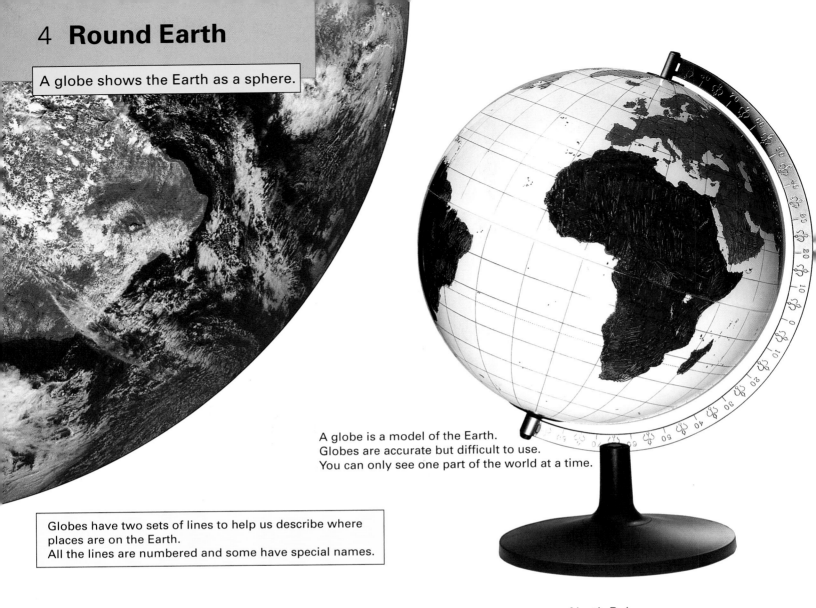

A globe is a model of the Earth.
Globes are accurate but difficult to use.
You can only see one part of the world at a time.

Globes have two sets of lines to help us describe where places are on the Earth.
All the lines are numbered and some have special names.

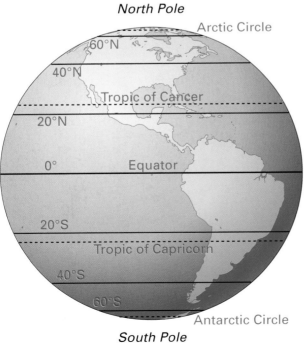

These are lines of latitude.

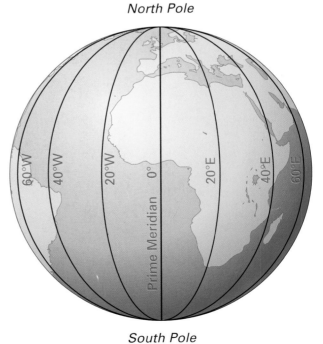

These are lines of longitude.

A world map shows the Earth on a flat piece of paper.

It is difficult to show shapes from a round Earth on a flat map.

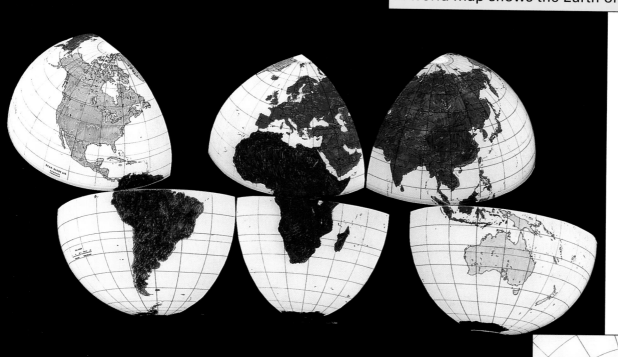

Most world maps do not show Antarctica clearly.

Not all world maps look the same.
There are differences in the shapes and sizes of the continents.
The patterns made by the lines of latitude and longitude are different.
Compare each world map with a globe.

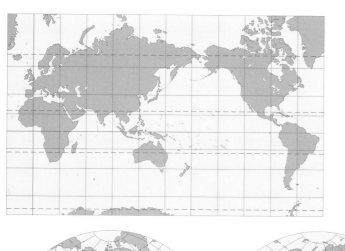

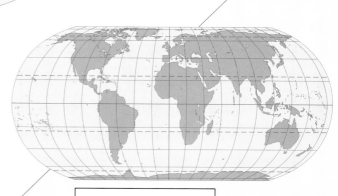

This is the world map used in this atlas.

6 Scale

Atlas maps have to be much, much smaller than the countries they show.

One centimetre on a map has to stand for many kilometres on the ground.

12 km

one cm

Every map in this atlas has a sign like this :

One centimetre on a map with *this* sign would stand for 12 kilometres on the ground.

You can see more detail on some maps than others. The amount of detail depends on the **scale** of the map.
See how the British Isles become smaller as the scale changes on the maps below.

Luton Welwyn Garden City Harlow
CHILTERN HILLS St Albans Chelmsford
Watford R. Lea Basildon
Slough London Southend-on-sea
Windsor Reading R. Medway NORTH
Woking Reigate Redhill Maidstone DOWNS
Guildford Crawley Ashford

Scale

20 km

one cm

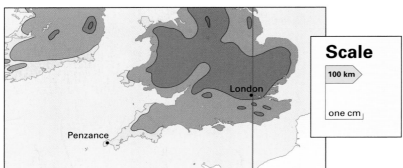

London
Penzance

Scale

100 km

one cm

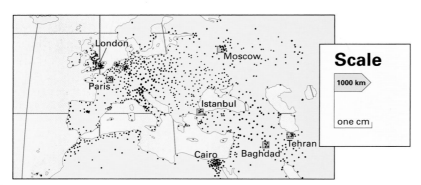

London Moscow
Paris Istanbul
Cairo Baghdad Tehran

Scale

1000 km

one cm

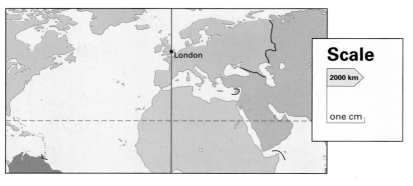

London

Scale

2000 km

one cm

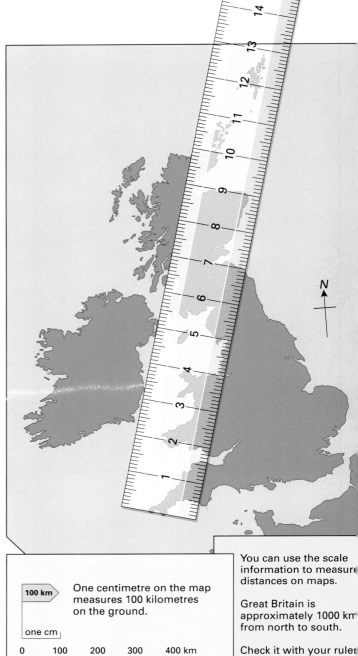

N

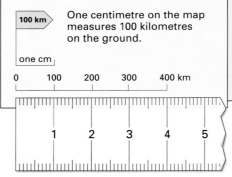

100 km

one cm

One centimetre on the map measures 100 kilometres on the ground.

0   100   200   300   400 km

1   2   3   4   5

You can use the scale information to measure distances on maps.

Great Britain is approximately 1000 km from north to south.

Check it with your ruler.

Small maps like this on some pages of the atlas help you to compare the size of other countries with the British Isles.

Most people in Britain live in towns.
Some towns are large, others are small.
In many parts of the country several towns have grown so large that they have joined to form one huge built-up area.

Each size of settlement has its own map symbol and style of lettering for the place name. Only the largest settlements are marked on atlas maps.

People live in settlements of different sizes.

Leeds

■ **Largest towns**
100 000 - 1 million people

Walsall
Sutton Coldfield
West Bromwich
Birmingham
Warley
Solihull
Kenilworth

Largest built-up areas
more than 1 million people

Bath R. Avon

● **Large towns**
25 000 - 100 000 people

752m ▲
Pumlumon
Aberystwyth

• **Small towns**
10 000 - 25 000 people

· **Small towns and villages**
fewer than 10 000 people

Many very small towns and villages are not shown on atlas maps.

On atlas maps the height of the land above sea level is shown by colours.

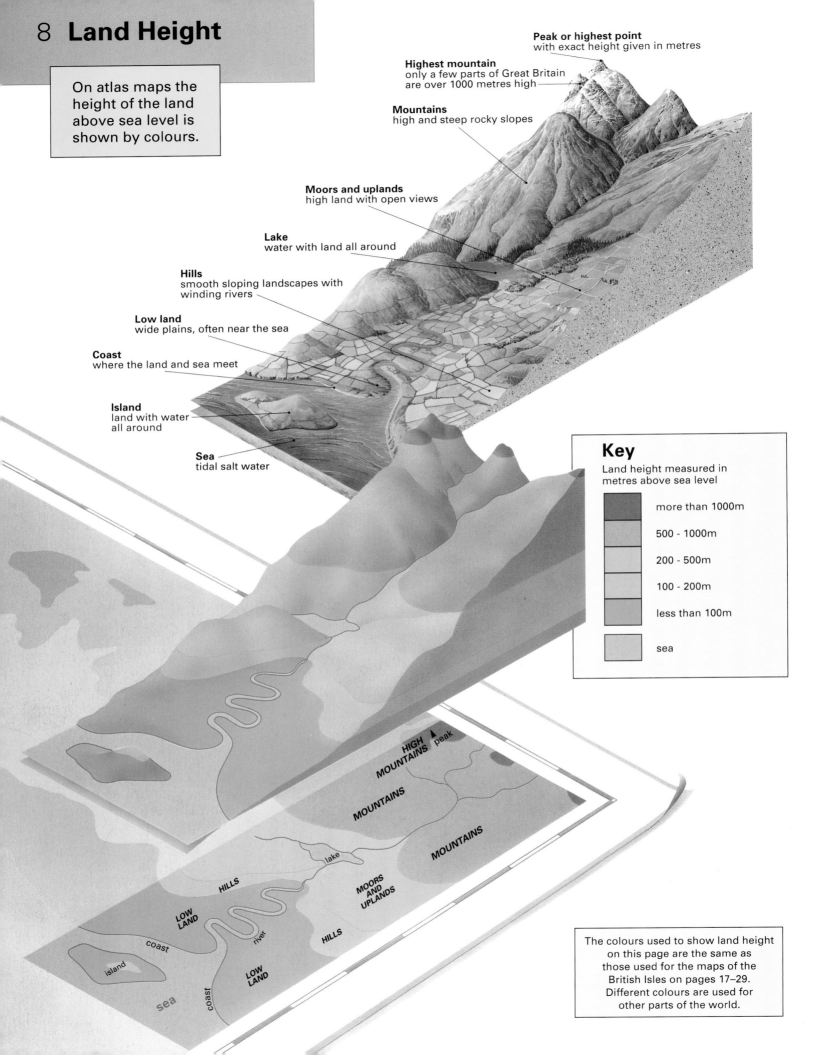

Peak or highest point
with exact height given in metres

Highest mountain
only a few parts of Great Britain
are over 1000 metres high

Mountains
high and steep rocky slopes

Moors and uplands
high land with open views

Lake
water with land all around

Hills
smooth sloping landscapes with
winding rivers

Low land
wide plains, often near the sea

Coast
where the land and sea meet

Island
land with water
all around

Sea
tidal salt water

Key
Land height measured in
metres above sea level

more than 1000m

500 - 1000m

200 - 500m

100 - 200m

less than 100m

sea

HIGH
MOUNTAINS ▲ peak

MOUNTAINS

lake

MOUNTAINS

HILLS

MOORS
AND
UPLANDS

LOW
LAND

HILLS

river

coast

LOW
LAND

island

coast

sea

The colours used to show land height
on this page are the same as
those used for the maps of the
British Isles on pages 17–29.
Different colours are used for
other parts of the world.

Rivers 9

Most landscapes in Great Britain have been shaped by rivers.

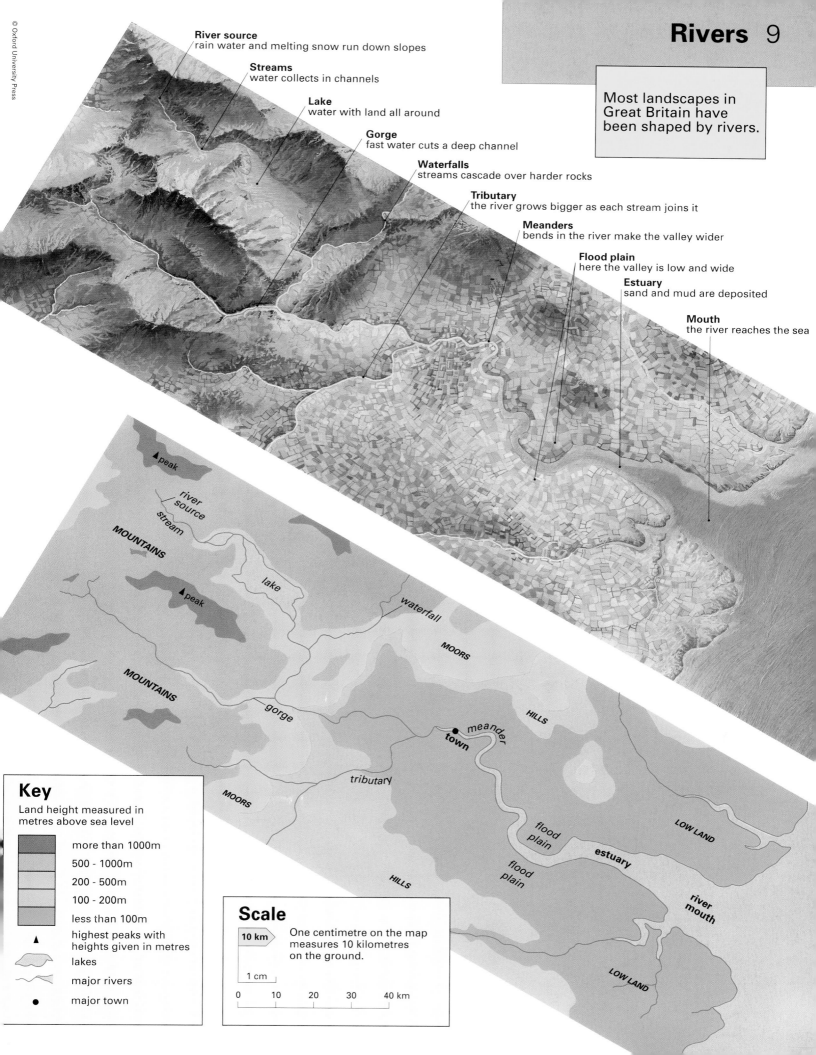

River source
rain water and melting snow run down slopes

Streams
water collects in channels

Lake
water with land all around

Gorge
fast water cuts a deep channel

Waterfalls
streams cascade over harder rocks

Tributary
the river grows bigger as each stream joins it

Meanders
bends in the river make the valley wider

Flood plain
here the valley is low and wide

Estuary
sand and mud are deposited

Mouth
the river reaches the sea

peak
river source
stream
MOUNTAINS
lake
MOUNTAINS
peak
waterfall
MOORS
gorge
HILLS
meander
town
tributary
MOORS
flood plain
flood plain
estuary
HILLS
LOW LAND
river mouth
LOW LAND

Key

Land height measured in metres above sea level

more than 1000m

500 - 1000m

200 - 500m

100 - 200m

less than 100m

▲ highest peaks with heights given in metres

lakes

major rivers

● major town

Scale

10 km One centimetre on the map measures 10 kilometres on the ground.

1 cm

0   10   20   30   40 km

A country is a land with its own people and its own government.

Scale

1050 km

One centimetre on the map measures 1050 kilometres on the ground at the Equator.

1 cm

| 0 | 1050 | 2100 | 3150 | 4200 km |

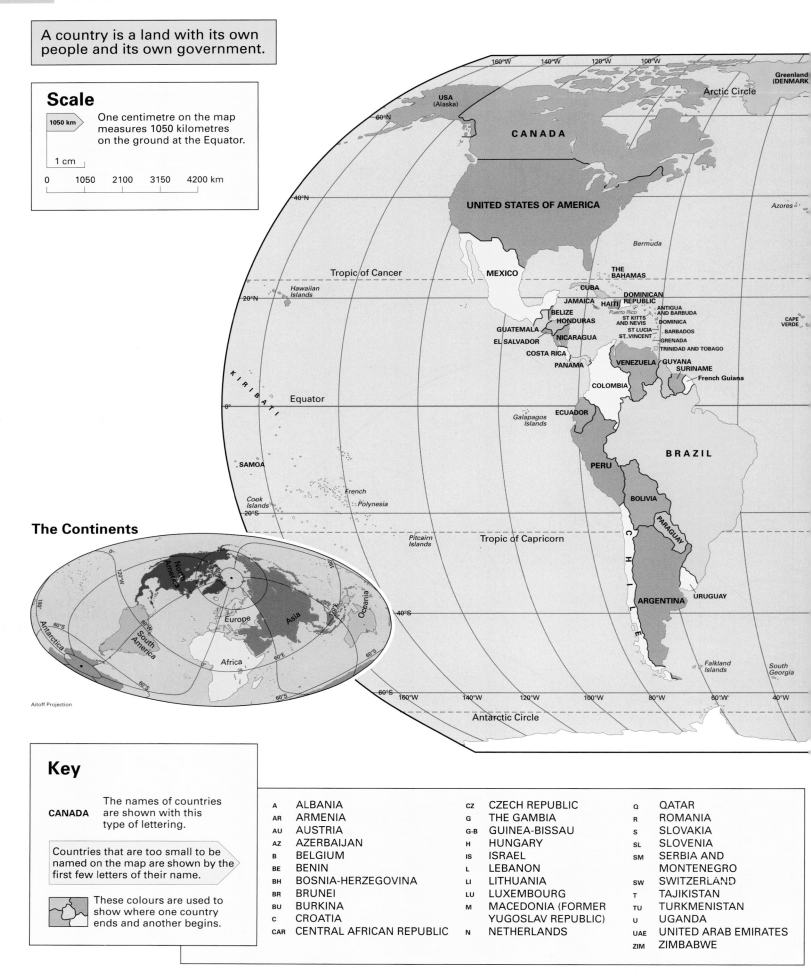

The Continents

Aitoff Projection

Key

CANADA The names of countries are shown with this type of lettering.

Countries that are too small to be named on the map are shown by the first few letters of their name.

These colours are used to show where one country ends and another begins.

A	ALBANIA	CZ	CZECH REPUBLIC	Q	QATAR
AR	ARMENIA	G	THE GAMBIA	R	ROMANIA
AU	AUSTRIA	G-B	GUINEA-BISSAU	S	SLOVAKIA
AZ	AZERBAIJAN	H	HUNGARY	SL	SLOVENIA
B	BELGIUM	IS	ISRAEL	SM	SERBIA AND
BE	BENIN	L	LEBANON		MONTENEGRO
BH	BOSNIA-HERZEGOVINA	LI	LITHUANIA	SW	SWITZERLAND
BR	BRUNEI	LU	LUXEMBOURG	T	TAJIKISTAN
BU	BURKINA	M	MACEDONIA (FORMER	TU	TURKMENISTAN
C	CROATIA		YUGOSLAV REPUBLIC)	U	UGANDA
CAR	CENTRAL AFRICAN REPUBLIC	N	NETHERLANDS	UAE	UNITED ARAB EMIRATES
				ZIM	ZIMBABWE

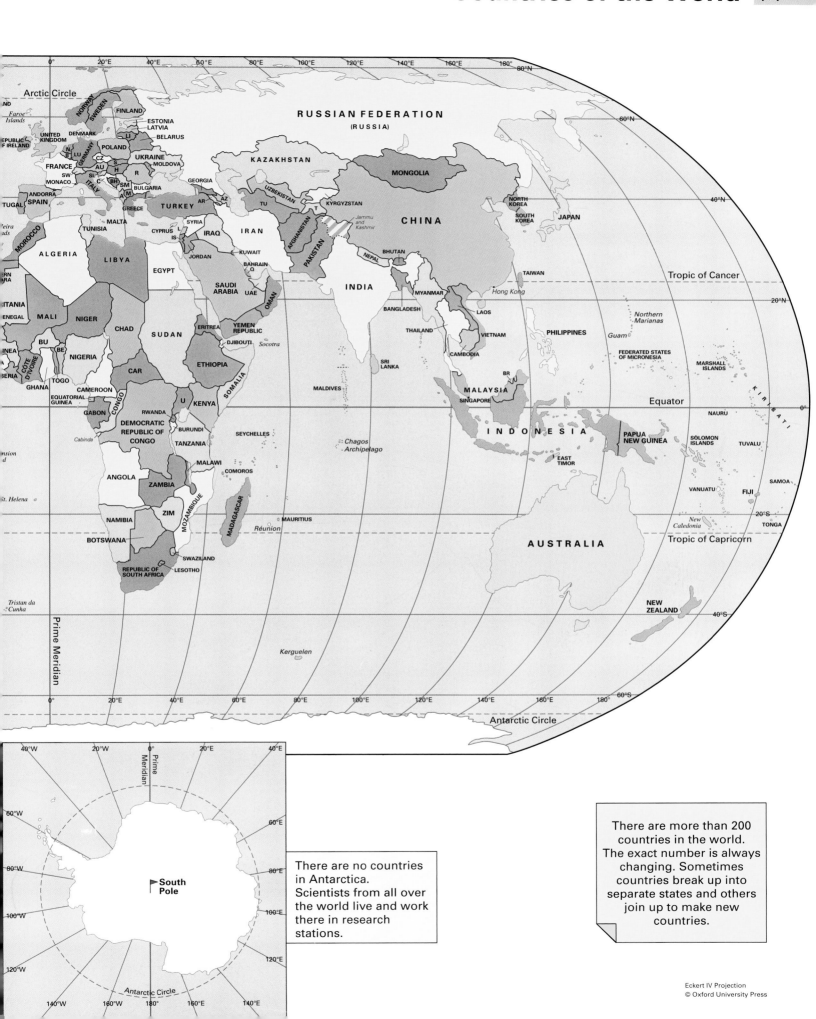

Arctic Circle

RUSSIAN FEDERATION
(RUSSIA)

NORWAY
SWEDEN
FINLAND
ESTONIA
LATVIA
DENMARK
BELARUS
LI
UNITED
KINGDOM
POLAND
REPUBLIC
OF IRELAND
N
B
LU
GERMANY
FRANCE
S
H
UKRAINE
KAZAKHSTAN
MONGOLIA
AU
MOLDOVA
MONACO
SL C
R
BH
SM
ANDORRA
A
M
BULGARIA
GEORGIA
UZBEKISTAN
KYRGYZSTAN
NORTH
KOREA
ITALY
SPAIN
GREECE
TURKEY
AR
AZ
TU
T
SOUTH
KOREA
JAPAN
TUGAL
MALTA
SYRIA
AFGHANISTAN
CHINA
MOROCCO
TUNISIA
CYPRUS
L
IS
IRAQ
IRAN
Jammu
and
Kashmir
Meira
ads
ALGERIA
LIBYA
JORDAN
KUWAIT
PAKISTAN
NEPAL
BHUTAN
Tropic of Cancer
TAIWAN
RN
RA
EGYPT
BAHRAIN
Q
SAUDI
ARABIA
UAE
INDIA
MYANMAR
Hong Kong
ITANIA
MALI
NIGER
CHAD
SUDAN
ERITREA
YEMEN
REPUBLIC
OMAN
BANGLADESH
LAOS
ENEGAL
DJIBOUTI
Socotra
THAILAND
VIETNAM
PHILIPPINES
Guam
FEDERATED STATES
OF MICRONESIA
MARSHALL
ISLANDS
BU
BE
NIGERIA
CAR
ETHIOPIA
SRI
LANKA
CAMBODIA
BR
INEA
COTE
D'IVOIRE
TOGO
GHANA
CAMEROON
MALDIVES
MALAYSIA
SINGAPORE
Equator
ERIA
EQUATORIAL
GUINEA
GABON
CONGO
U
KENYA
SOMALIA
NAURU
DEMOCRATIC
REPUBLIC OF
CONGO
RWANDA
BURUNDI
TANZANIA
SEYCHELLES
Chagos
Archipelago
INDONESIA
PAPUA
NEW GUINEA
SOLOMON
ISLANDS
TUVALU
Cabinda
EAST
TIMOR
nsion
d
ANGOLA
ZAMBIA
MALAWI
COMOROS
SAMOA
St. Helena
ZIM
MOZAMBIQUE
MADAGASCAR
MAURITIUS
Réunion
20°S
VANUATU
FIJI
New
Caledonia
TONGA
NAMIBIA
BOTSWANA
SWAZILAND
LESOTHO
AUSTRALIA
Tropic of Capricorn
Tristan da
Cunha
REPUBLIC OF
SOUTH AFRICA
Prime Meridian
NEW
ZEALAND

Kerguelen

Antarctic Circle

South
Pole

There are no countries
in Antarctica.
Scientists from all over
the world live and work
there in research
stations.

There are more than 200
countries in the world.
The exact number is always
changing. Sometimes
countries break up into
separate states and others
join up to make new
countries.

Eckert IV Projection
© Oxford University Press

England, Scotland, and Wales, together with Northern Ireland, form the United Kingdom. The Republic of Ireland is a separate country.

England is divided into counties and some new unitary authorities. Wa[...] and Scotland are divid[...] into unitary authorities[...] Northern Ireland is divided into districts.

The Republic of Irelan[...] divided into counties.

Scale

45 km

One centimetre on the map measures 45 kilometres on the ground

1 cm

0   45   90   135   180 km

Key to unitary authorities in Scotland

1 West Dunbartonshire
2 East Dunbartonshire
3 North Lanarkshire
4 Glasgow City
5 East Renfrewshire
6 Renfrewshire
7 Inverclyde
8 Clackmannanshire
9 Falkirk
10 West Lothian
11 City of Edinburgh
12 Midlothian
13 East Lothian
14 North Ayrshire
15 East Ayrshire
16 Dundee City

Key to districts in Northern Ireland

1 Belfast	14 Fermanagh
2 Newtownabbey	15 Omagh
3 Carrickfergus	16 Cookstown
4 Castlereagh	17 Magherafelt
5 North Down	18 Strabane
6 Ards	19 Derry
7 Down	20 Limavady
8 Newry & Mourne	21 Coleraine
9 Banbridge	22 Ballymoney
10 Lisburn	23 Moyle
11 Craigavon	24 Ballymena
12 Armagh	25 Larne
13 Dungannon	26 Antrim

The British Isles consis[...] of the two large island[...] of Great Britain and Ireland and a number of smaller islands.

Key to unitary authorities in Wales

1 Cardiff	8 Caerphilly
2 The Vale of Glamorgan	9 Blaenau Gwent
3 Bridgend	10 Monmouthshire
4 Swansea	11 Conwy
5 Neath Port Talbot	12 Denbighshire
6 Rhondda Cynon Taff	13 Flintshire
7 Merthyr Tydfil	14 Wrexham

Key to unitary authorities in England

1 Hartlepool	10 Bristol
2 Stockton-on-Tees	11 North Somerset
3 Middlesbrough	12 Bath and North East Somerset
4 Redcar and Cleveland	13 Luton
5 East Riding of Yorkshire	14 Milton Keynes
6 City of Kingston upon Hull	15 Leicester City
7 North Lincolnshire	16 Swindon
8 North East Lincolnshire	17 Windsor & Maidenhead
9 South Gloucestershire	

Transverse Mercator Projection
© Oxford University Press

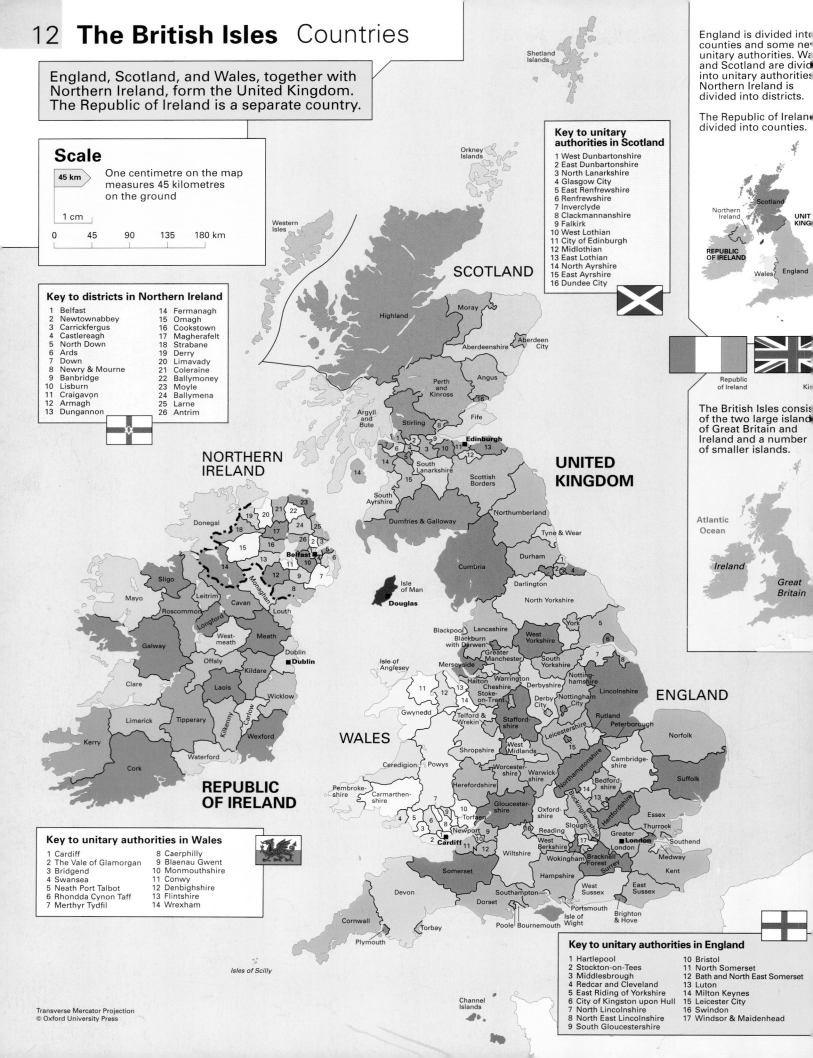

The British Isles Land height and rivers

The highest parts of Great Britain are mostly in the north and west.

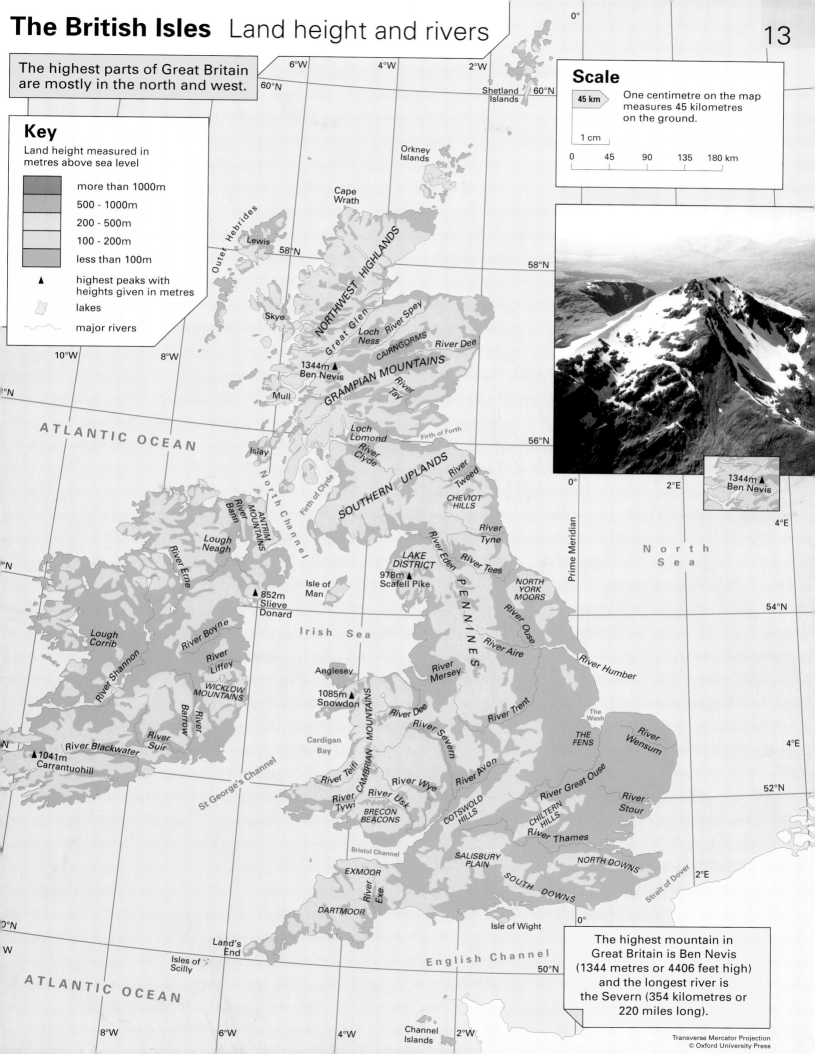

Key

Land height measured in metres above sea level

- more than 1000m
- 500 - 1000m
- 200 - 500m
- 100 - 200m
- less than 100m

▲ highest peaks with heights given in metres

lakes

major rivers

Scale

45 km → One centimetre on the map measures 45 kilometres on the ground.

1 cm

0   45   90   135   180 km

1344m ▲ Ben Nevis

The highest mountain in Great Britain is Ben Nevis (1344 metres or 4406 feet high) and the longest river is the Severn (354 kilometres or 220 miles long).

Transverse Mercator Projection
© Oxford University Press

Labels on map:

Shetland Islands, Orkney Islands, Cape Wrath, Outer Hebrides, Lewis, Skye, Mull, Islay, NORTHWEST HIGHLANDS, Great Glen, Loch Ness, River Spey, CAIRNGORMS, River Dee, 1344m ▲ Ben Nevis, GRAMPIAN MOUNTAINS, River Tay, Loch Lomond, River Clyde, Firth of Forth, Firth of Clyde, SOUTHERN UPLANDS, River Tweed, CHEVIOT HILLS, River Tyne, River Eden, River Tees, LAKE DISTRICT, 978m ▲ Scafell Pike, NORTH YORK MOORS, River Ouse, PENNINES, River Aire, River Humber, River Mersey, River Trent, The Wash, THE FENS, River Wensum, River Great Ouse, River Stour, CHILTERN HILLS, River Avon, COTSWOLD HILLS, River Thames, NORTH DOWNS, Strait of Dover, SALISBURY PLAIN, SOUTH DOWNS, Isle of Wight, River Exe, EXMOOR, DARTMOOR, Land's End, Isles of Scilly, English Channel, Channel Islands, Bristol Channel, BRECON BEACONS, River Usk, River Wye, River Severn, River Dee, CAMBRIAN MOUNTAINS, 1085m ▲ Snowdon, Anglesey, Cardigan Bay, River Teifi, River Tywi, St George's Channel, Isle of Man, Irish Sea, North Channel, ANTRIM MOUNTAINS, River Bann, Lough Neagh, River Erne, Lough Corrib, River Shannon, River Boyne, River Liffey, WICKLOW MOUNTAINS, River Barrow, River Suir, River Blackwater, ▲1041m Carrantuohill, 852m ▲ Slieve Donard, ATLANTIC OCEAN, North Sea, Prime Meridian

60°N, 58°N, 56°N, 54°N, 52°N, 50°N, 10°W, 8°W, 6°W, 4°W, 2°W, 0°, 2°E, 4°E

Climate describes the average pattern of weather over a number of years.

During the year many wet weather fronts pass over the British Isles whilst southern Europe stays dry and warm. This is a satellite picture of the weather in western Europe on 6 August 1987.
Satellite pictures like this use colours that are different from the way the land looks to us.

Transverse Mercator Projection
© Oxford University Press

Rainfall

The eastern parts of the British Isles are drier than the western parts. Mountains are wetter than lowlands.

Average annual rainfall

The graphs show the amount of rainfall in Blaenau Ffestiniog and London for one year.
Blaenau Ffestiniog is wetter in winter.
London has about the same amount of rainfall each month.

All the rain that falls in one year is the **annual rainfall**. Blaenau Ffestiniog has much more rain than London over the whole year.

Some years are wetter than others. The map shows the amount of rainfall you would expect in an average year.

Average annual rainfall in millimetres

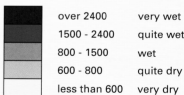

	over 2400	very wet
	1500 - 2400	quite wet
	800 - 1500	wet
	600 - 800	quite dry
	less than 600	very dry

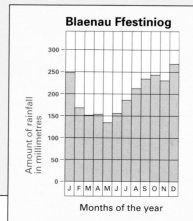

Blaenau Ffestiniog

London

Months of the year

Months of the year

January temperatures

In winter the mountains of Scotland are the coldest parts of the British Isles.

July temperatures

In summer the coasts of southern England are the warmest parts of the British Isles.

Scale

100 km

One centimetre on the map measures 100 kilometres on the ground.

1 cm

100   200   300   400 km

In the British Isles it is usually colder in January than in July. However, some years might be very cold whilst others are quite warm. The maps show the temperatures you would expect in an average year.

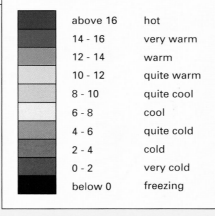

Average temperatures in °Celsius

	above 16	hot
	14 - 16	very warm
	12 - 14	warm
	10 - 12	quite warm
	8 - 10	quite cool
	6 - 8	cool
	4 - 6	quite cold
	2 - 4	cold
	0 - 2	very cold
	below 0	freezing

Average temperatures in winter and summer

The graphs show the average temperatures each month for Stornoway, Braemar, London, and Valley.
In all four places it is warmer in summer than in winter.

Summers in Stornoway and Braemar are much cooler than in London or Valley.
Winter in Braemar is very cold.

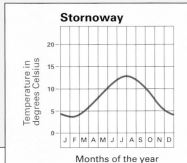

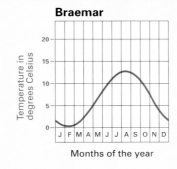

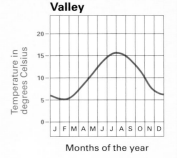

Transverse Mercator Projection
© Oxford University Press

Maps that show all the most important features of the landscape are called **topographic** maps.

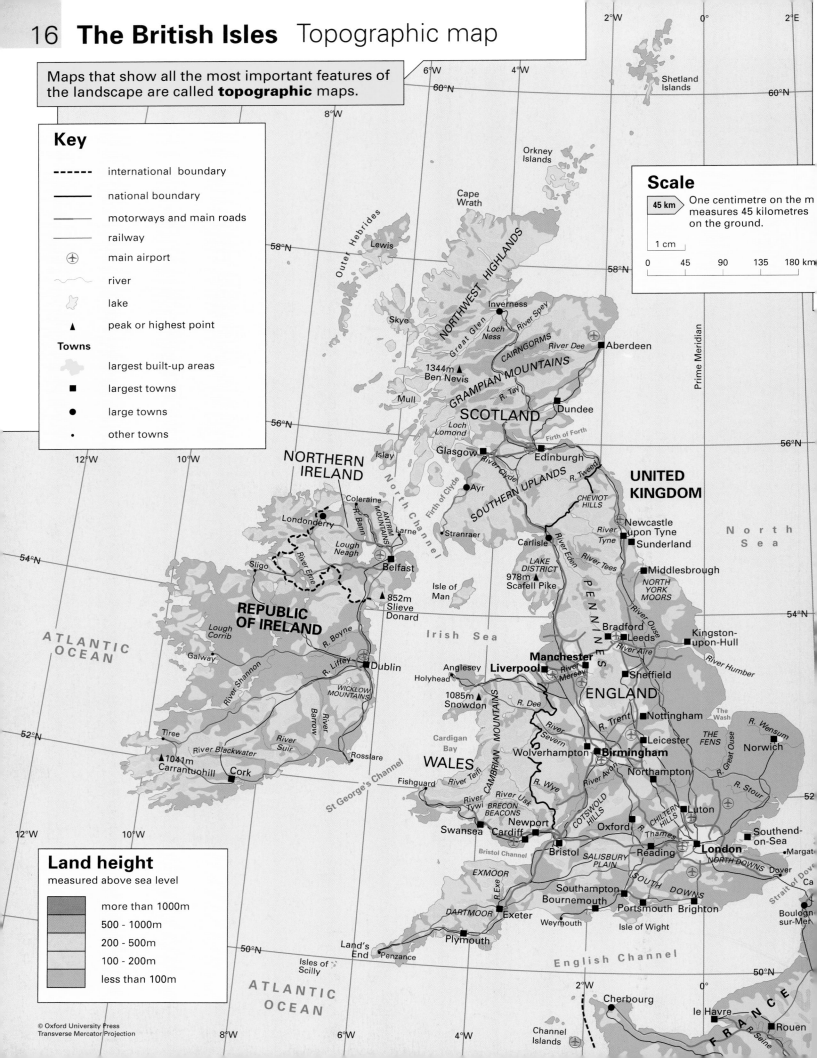

Key

- - - - -	international boundary
——	national boundary
——	motorways and main roads
——	railway
⊕	main airport
∿	river
	lake
▲	peak or highest point

Towns

	largest built-up areas
■	largest towns
●	large towns
•	other towns

Scale

One centimetre on the m measures 45 kilometres on the ground.

45 km

1 cm

0   45   90   135   180 km

Land height
measured above sea level

	more than 1000m
	500 - 1000m
	200 - 500m
	100 - 200m
	less than 100m

Shetland Islands

Orkney Islands

Cape Wrath

Lewis

Outer Hebrides

Skye

NORTHWEST HIGHLANDS

Inverness

Great Glen

Loch Ness

River Spey

CAIRNGORMS

River Dee

Aberdeen

1344m ▲ Ben Nevis

GRAMPIAN MOUNTAINS

Mull

R. Tay

SCOTLAND

Dundee

Loch Lomond

Firth of Forth

Glasgow

River Clyde

Edinburgh

Islay

Ayr

SOUTHERN UPLANDS

R. Tweed

CHEVIOT HILLS

UNITED KINGDOM

Coleraine

R. Bann

ANTRIM MOUNTAINS

Larne

Stranraer

Carlisle

River Eden

River Tyne

Newcastle upon Tyne

Sunderland

NORTHERN IRELAND

Londonderry

Lough Neagh

Belfast

River Erne

Sligo

River Tees

LAKE DISTRICT

978m ▲ Scafell Pike

Middlesbrough

NORTH YORK MOORS

▲ 852m Slieve Donard

Isle of Man

North Channel

Irish Sea

PENNINES

REPUBLIC OF IRELAND

Lough Corrib

R. Boyne

Bradford

Leeds

Kingston-upon-Hull

Galway

River Shannon

R. Liffey

Dublin

River Ouse

River Aire

Anglesey

Manchester

Liverpool

River Mersey

Sheffield

River Humber

WICKLOW MOUNTAINS

Holyhead

ENGLAND

Tiree

River Blackwater

River Suir

Barrow

River

Rosslare

1085m ▲ Snowdon

R. Dee

Nottingham

The Wash

R. Wensum

▲ 1041m Carrantuohill

Cork

R. Trent

Leicester

THE FENS

Norwich

Fishguard

River Teifi

CAMBRIAN MOUNTAINS

River Severn

River Avon

Northampton

R. Great Ouse

R. Stour

WALES

Cardigan Bay

Wolverhampton

Birmingham

Luton

St George's Channel

River Tywi

BRECON BEACONS

River Usk

R. Wye

COTSWOLD HILLS

Oxford

CHILTERN HILLS

Southend-on-Sea

Swansea

Newport

Cardiff

R. Thames

Reading

London

Margat

Bristol Channel

Bristol

SALISBURY PLAIN

NORTH DOWNS

Dover

Strait of Dove

EXMOOR

R.Exe

Southampton

Bournemouth

SOUTH DOWNS

Portsmouth

Brighton

Ca

DARTMOOR

Exeter

Weymouth

Isle of Wight

Boulogne-sur-Mer

Land's End

Penzance

Plymouth

Isles of Scilly

ATLANTIC OCEAN

English Channel

Cherbourg

le Havre

Channel Islands

FRANCE

Rouen

R. Seine

ATLANTIC OCEAN

North Sea

Prime Meridian

3°W C 2°W D 1°W E

Herma Ness

Haroldswick

Unst

ATLANTIC

Point of
Fethaland

Yell Sound

Yell *Fetlar*

▲ 449m

3

Esha Ness

*Out
Skerries*

OCEAN

St Magnus
Bay

*Muckle
Roe*

Whalsay
Symbister

*Papa
Stour*

Mainland **SHETLAND
ISLANDS**

Walls

Bressay

417m
Foula ▲

The
Deeps

Lerwick

Scalloway

60°N 60°N

Sumburgh
Head

Scale

10 km ▷ One centimetre on the map
measures 10 kilometres
on the ground.

1 cm

0 10 20 30 40 km

3

Key

– – – – county or region boundary

——— motorway and main roads

——— railway

⊕ main airport

river

lake

▲ peak or highest point

• towns

Land height

measured above sea level

200-500m

100-200m

less than 100m

4°W

B

2

Fair Isle

2

Mull Head

Papa Westray

North Ronaldsay

Westray

Sanday

Westray Firth

Rousay

Eday

Brough Head

Stronsay

Stronsay Firth

Shapinsay

°N

Stromness

Mainland

Kirkwall

Scapa

**ORKNEY
ISLANDS**

1°W

59°N

Kirkwall

Ward Hill
479m ▲

*Scapa
Flow*

Rora Head

Hoy

South Ronaldsay

1

Pentland Firth

Stroma

North Sea

Dunnet Head

Strathy
Point

John o' Groats

Duncansby Head

1

A 4°W **B** 3°W **C** 2°W **D** Transverse Mercator Projection **E**
© Oxford University Press

Thurso

Halkirk

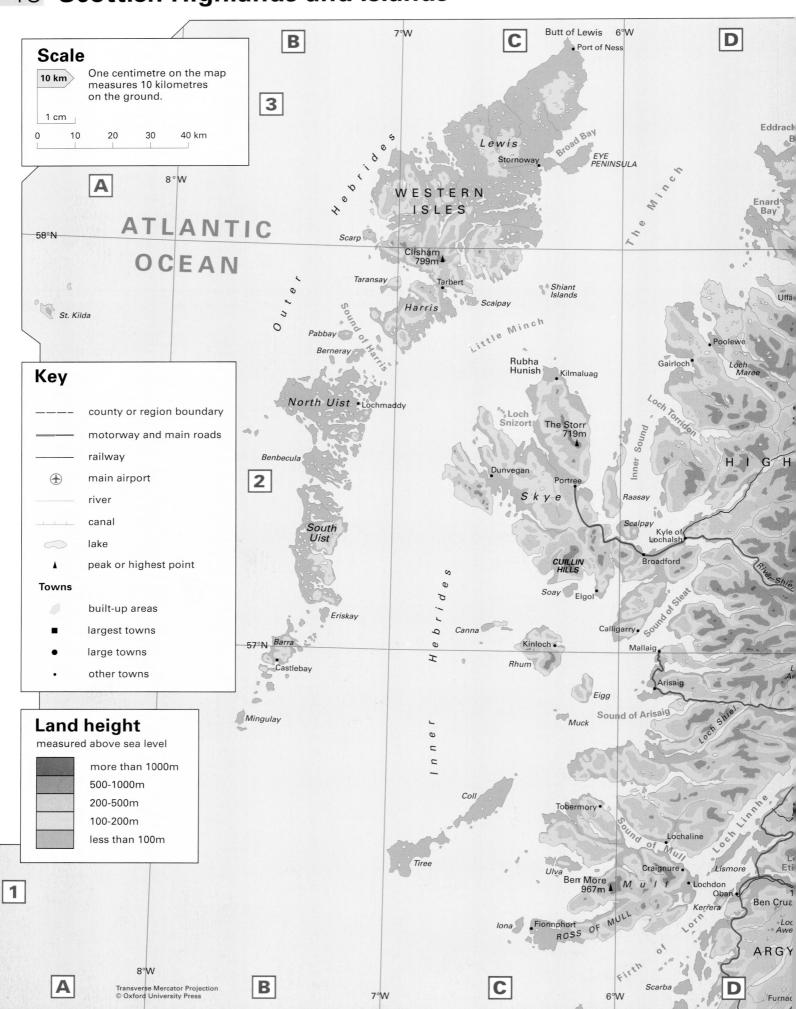

Scale

10 km One centimetre on the map measures 10 kilometres on the ground.

1 cm

0   10   20   30   40 km

Key

– – – – –	county or region boundary
━━━━━	motorway and main roads
———	railway
⊕	main airport
———	river
┼┼┼┼┼	canal
⬭	lake
▲	peak or highest point

Towns

▨	built-up areas
■	largest towns
●	large towns
•	other towns

Land height

measured above sea level

	more than 1000m
	500-1000m
	200-500m
	100-200m
	less than 100m

ATLANTIC
OCEAN

St. Kilda

Butt of Lewis
Port of Ness

Lewis
Stornoway
Broad Bay
EYE PENINSULA

WESTERN ISLES

The Minch

Eddrach
B

Enard Bay

Hebrides

Outer

Scarp
Clisham 799m▲

Taransay
Tarbert
Harris
Scalpay
Shiant Islands

Ulfa
Poolewe
Gairloch
Loch Maree

Sound of Harris

Pabbay
Berneray

Little Minch

Rubha Hunish
Kilmaluag

Loch Torridon

North Uist •Lochmaddy

Loch Snizort
The Storr 719m▲

Inner Sound

H I G H

Benbecula

Dunvegan
Skye
Portree
Raasay

South Uist

Scalpay
Kyle of Lochalsh

CUILLIN HILLS
Broadford

Eriskay

Hebrides

Canna

Soay
Elgol

Sound of Sleat

River Shiel

Barra

Kinloch
Rhum

Calligarry
Mallaig

Castlebay

Inner

Arisaig
L
Ar

Mingulay

Eigg

Sound of Arisaig
Loch Shiel

Muck

Coll

Tobermory

Ulva
Iona
Fionnphort
Tiree
Ben More 967m▲
Mull
ROSS OF MULL

Sound of Mull
Lochaline
Craignure
Lismore
Lochdon
Oban
Kerrera

Loch Linnhe
L
Eti

Ben Crua

ARGY

Firth of Lorn

Scarba
Furnac

Loch Awe

58°N

57°N

8°W   7°W   6°W

Key

- –·–·–·– international boundary
- – – – national boundary
- – · – county or region boundary
- ▬▬ motorway and main roads
- ──── railway
- ✈ main airport
- ──── river
- ──┼── canal
- ◯ lake
- ▲ peak or highest point

Towns
- built-up areas
- ■ largest towns
- ● large towns
- · other towns

Land height
measured above sea level

- more than 1000m
- 500-1000m
- 200-500m
- 100-200m
- less than 100m

4

3

Belfast Edinburgh

56°N

7°W

A 8°W **B**

Malin Head

Tory Island
Tory Sound

3

Errigal Mountain 752m
Creeslough
Kilmacrenan
Letterkenny
R. Swilly
Ballybofey

55°N

DONEGAL
River Finn

Donegal
River Derg

Ballyshannon

2

Lough Melvin

FERMANAGH
Lough Macnean Upper
Lough Macnean Lower

LEITRIM
Shannon
Lough Allen

R. Erne
Upper Lough Erne
Clones

CAVAN
Lough Oughter
Cavan

REPUBLIC OF IRELAND

8°W **B** 7°W

INISHOWEN PENINSULA
Slieve Snaght 615m
Buncrana
Lough Swilly

Lough Foyle
River Foyle
Londonderry
DERRY
Strabane
STRABANE
Newtownstewart

Omagh
OMAGH

Lower Lough Erne
Enniskillen

Portrush
Portstewart
Coleraine
COLERAINE
Limavady
LIMAVADY
Dungiven
Sawel 683m

Maghera
MAGHERAFELT
Magherafelt
529m

Cookstown
COOKSTOWN

Dungannon
DUNGANNON
Coalisland

MONAGHAN
Monaghan
Castleblayney
Crossmaglen

Ballycastle
MOYLE
Rathlin Island
Rathlin Sound
Fair Head

River Bush
Ballymoney
BALLYMONEY
River Bann
River Main
BALLYMENA
Ballymena
ANTRIM MOUNTAINS
LARNE Larne

Lough Beg
ANTRIM
Randalstown
Antrim

Lough Neagh
Crumlin

R. Blackwater
CRAIGAVON
Lurgan
Portadown
Craigavon

ARMAGH
Armagh
Keady
Newtownhamilton

NEWRY AND MOURNE
Newry
Warrenpoint
Crossmaglen

C

Iona
Fionnphort ROSS OF MULL
Scarba

Colonsay
Scalasaig
Oronsay

Port Askaig
Craighouse

I s l a y
Portnahaven
Port Ellen
Ardbeg
Mull of Oa

6°W

Firth of Lorn

J u r a
Sound of Jura

Kilmory
Gigha
Ardminish

KINTYRE

Campbeltown

Southend
Mull of Kintyre

North Channel

M2
NEWTOWNABBEY
Newtownabbey
BELFAST
Belfast
Lisburn
LISBURN
M1
CARRICKFERGUS
Carrickfergus
Island Magee
Belfast Lough
CASTLEREAGH
NORTH DOWN
Bangor
Donaghadee
Newtownards
ARDS
Strangford Lough
ARDS PENINSULA

Dromore
Banbridge
River Bann
BANBRIDGE
D O W N
Downpatrick

Slieve Donard 852m
Newcastle
St John's Point

Kilkeel

Carlingford Lough

D 5°W

Oban
Dalmally
Loch Awe
Kerrera
Inveraray
ARGYLL AND BU
Furnace
Loch Fyne
Lochgilphead
Dunoo
Tighnabruaich
Bute
Rothesay
Clachan
Claonaig Sound of Bute
Lochranza
Goat Fell 874m ▲
Arran Brodick
NORTH AYRSHIRE

Ailsa Craig
Ballantrae

Corsewall Point

Stranraer
Portpatrick

Drummor
Mull of Galloway

54°N

7°W **C** LOUTH
Dundalk

6°W **D** 5°W

Transverse Mercator Projection
© Oxford University Press

Scale

10 km

One centimetre on the map measures 10 kilometres on the ground.

1 cm

0   10   20   30   40 km

Transverse Mercator Projection
© Oxford University Press

4   B   C   2°W   D   Bly Cramlingt

NORTHUMBERLAND

Newcastle upon Tyne

Gateshead

Washingt

Chester-le-Street

Conset

Durham

Glenluce   Newton Stewart   Castle   Kirkbean   55°N   River Irthing   Haltwhistle   Hexham   R. Tyne

Wigtown   Gatehouse of Fleet   Dalbeattie   Kirkcudbright   Carlisle   Brampton

R. Dee   Wigton   Penrith   Cross Fell 893m   River Wear   DURHAM   Spennymoor

Luce Bay   Wigtown Bay   Solway Firth   Maryport   River Ellen   R. Derwent   Cockermouth   931m Skiddaw   CUMBRIA   Mickle Fell 790m   Appleby-in-Westmorland   Bishop Auckland   Newton Aycliffe

Mull of Galloway   Workington   Keswick   Derwent Water   Ullswater   Brough   Barnard Castle   DARLINGT   Darlington

Whitehaven   Helvellyn 950m   LAKE   Kirkby Stephen   Richmond

St Bees Head   DISTRICT   Ambleside   River Swale

Point of Ayre   Seascale   978m Scafell Pike   Windermere   Windermere   NORTH

Ramsey   Coniston Water   R. Ure   Leyburn

Kirk Michael   Snaefell 620m   Kendal   Whernside 737m   River Wharfe   Leyburn

Peel   ISLE OF MAN   Great Whernside 704m   River Nidd   Rip

South Barrule 483m   Douglas   Barrow-in-Furness   Dalton-in-Furness   Morecambe Bay   Carnforth   723m Ingleborough   Pen-y-Ghent 693m

Castletown   Morecambe   Lancaster   560m Ward's Stone   River Nidd

54°N   Heysham   FOREST OF BOWLAND   River Aire   Skipton   Harroga

Fleetwood   River Wyre   Barnoldswick   Ilkley   Keighley

Irish Sea   BLACKPOOL   LANCASHIRE   River Ribble   Nelson   Bradford   Lee

Blackpool   M55   **Preston**   Burnley   Halifax   WEST

Lytham St Anne's   Leyland   Blackburn   BLACKBURN WITH DARWEN   Brighouse   Dewsbu

Southport   Chorley   **Huddersfield**   YORKSHIRE

Carmel Head   Amlwch   Formby   Skelmersdale   Wigan   **Bolton**   Bury   **Rochdale**   YORKSHIRE

Holyhead   ISLE OF ANGLESEY   Kirkby   GREATER MANCHESTER   **Oldham**

Holy Island   Langefni   Bootle   Wallasey   St Helens   **Manchester**

Llandudno   Rhyl   Prestatyn   MERSEYSIDE   **Salford**   **Stockport**   Kinder Scout 636m

Conwy   **Birkenhead**   **Liverpool**   **Warrington**   Sale

Bangor   Colwyn Bay   River Dee   Widnes   WARRINGTON   **Cheadle**

Bethesda   FLINTSHIRE   Flint   R. Mersey   **Runcorn**   Macclesfield   Buxton

Caernarfon   Denbigh   HALTON   Ellesmere Port   Northwich   CHESHIRE

Snowdon 1085m   CONWY   Mold   Chester   Winsford   Bakewell

Caernarfon Bay   R. Conwy   River Clwyd   DENBIGHSHIRE   DERBYSH

53°N   Blaenau Ffestiniog   Crewe   Kidsgrove   Matlock

LLŶN PENINSULA   Porthmadog   Wrexham   STOKE-ON-TRENT   **Stoke-on-Trent**

Pwllheli   Bala   WREXHAM   Newcastle-under-Lyme

Harlech   GWYNEDD   Bala Lake   Llangollen   **ENGLAND**

Lake Vyrnwy   River Dee   Whitchurch   Uttoxeter   DERBY C

Barmouth   CAMBRIAN MOUNTAINS   Oswestry   Market Drayton   M6   Burton upon Trent

Cader Idris 892m   POWYS   R. Vyrnwy   Newport   STAFFORDSHIRE   Stafford

Cardigan Bay   Dolgellau   WALES   Welshpool   Shrewsbury   TELFORD AND WREKIN   407m The Wrekin   **Telford**   Cannock   Rugeley

Machynlleth   R. Dyfi   SHROPSHIRE   3°W   M54   Lichfield

4°W   B   C   **Wolverhampton**   Tamworth   D

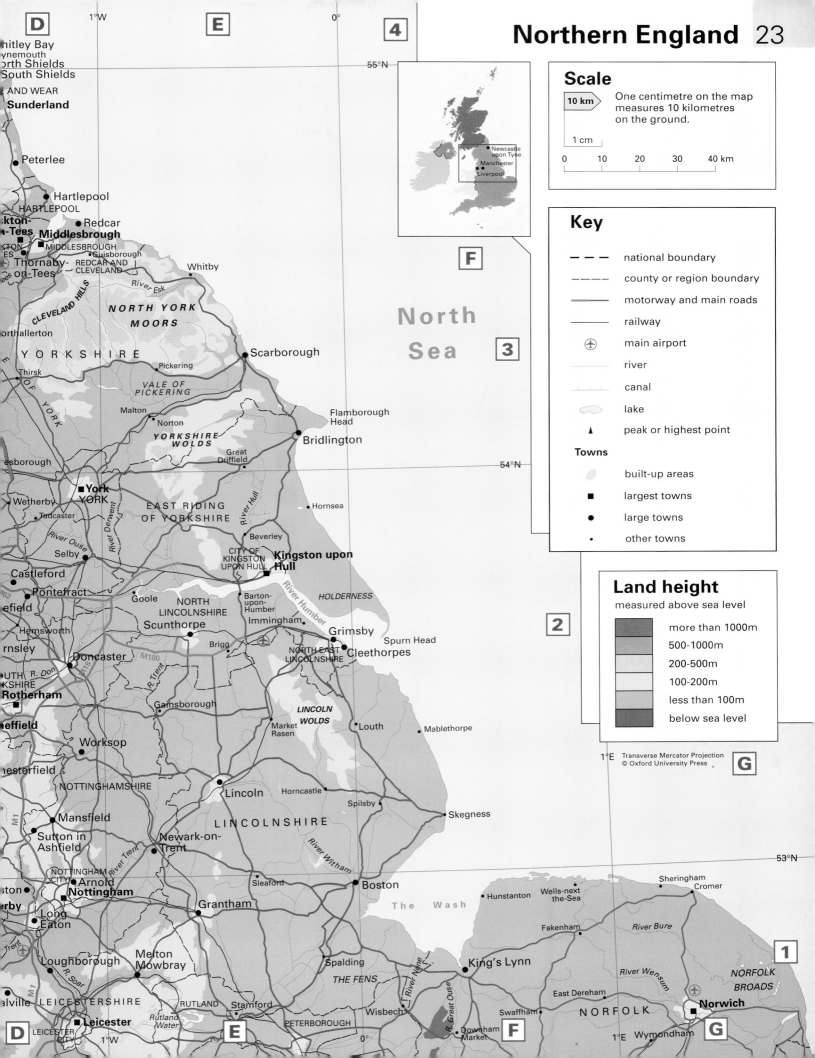

A 6°W
Malahide
Howth
Dublin
Dún Laoghaire
3
Bray
Greystones
REPUBLIC OF IRELAND
53°N
Wicklow
Arklow

B 5°W

C 4°W

D
Formby
MERSEYS
Bootle
Wallasey
Liverpo
Birkenhead

Carmel Head
Amlwch
Holyhead
Holy Island
ISLE OF ANGLESEY
Langefni
Bangor
Bethesda
Caernarfon
Snowdon 1085m

Llandudno Rhyl Prestatyn
Conwy Colwyn Bay
FLINTSHIRE
Flint
River Dee
WS3
Denbigh
Mold
DENBIGHSHIRE
Wrexham
WRE

Irish Sea

LLŶN PENINSULA
Porthmadog
Pwllheli
Harlech
Bardsey Island

Blaenau Ffestiniog

GWYNEDD
Barmouth
Dolgellau
Cader Idris 892m

CONWY

Bala
Bala Lake
Lake Vyrnwy

905m
Aran Fawddwy

Llangollen
River Dee
Oswestry

R. Vyrnwy

WALES
R. Dyfi
Machynlleth
R. Severn
Welshpool
Montgo

Cardigan Bay

2
52°N

752m
Plynlimon
Aberystwyth

Llanidloes
Newtown

CEREDIGION
Aberaeron
New Quay

CAMBRIAN
R. Severn

Rhayader
Knighton

Cemaes Head
Cardigan
River Teifi
Newcastle Emlyn

Lampeter

POWYS

Llandrindod Wells

Builth Wells
Kir

St George's Channel
Strumble Head
Fishguard
MYNYDD PRESELI

River Teifi

Llandovery

MYNYDD EPPYNT

R. Wye
Hay-on

St David's Head
St David's
PEMBROKESHIRE
Haverfordwest
St Brides Bay
Milford Haven
Pembroke
Tenby

CARMARTHENSHIRE
Carmarthen
Llandeilo

R. Tywi

River Usk
Brecon

811m
BLAC
MOUNTA

BRECON
886m
BEACONS

Abergavenny

Kidwelly
Burry Port
Carmarthen Bay

Ammanford
Pontardulais

Merthyr Tydfil
Aberdare
RHONDDA
MERTHYR TYDFIL

Ebbw Vale
BLAENAU GWENT
TORF
Abertillery
Pontypool
Cwmbran

1
ATLANTIC

OCEAN

Llanelli
Worms Head
GOWER
Swansea
SWANSEA
NEATH PORT TALBOT
Port Talbot
Neath
M4
Bridgend
THE VALE OF GLAMORGAN

CYNON
Rhondda
TAFF
Pontypridd
BRIDGEND

CAERPHILLY
Caerphilly
CARDIFF
Barry

Newpor
NEWF
CARDIFF
Cardiff

Bristol Channel

Weston-super-Mare

Bridgwater Bay

Ilfracombe
Lundy
C
DEVON 4°W EXMOOR
Lynton
Dunkery Beacon 519m
Minehead
D

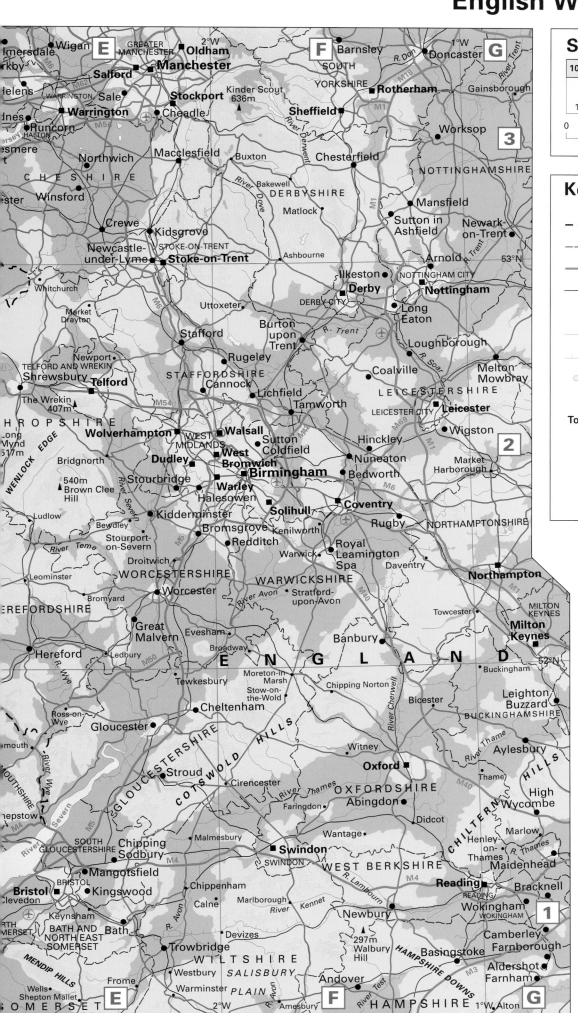

Scale

10 km ➤ One centimetre on the map measures 10 kilometres on the ground.

1 cm

0   10   20   30   40 km

Key

- – – – national boundary
- - - - - county or region boundary
- —— motorway and main roads
- —— railway
- ✈ main airport
- —— river
- ┼┼ canal
- 〰 lake
- ▲ peak or highest point

Towns

- built-up areas
- ■ largest towns
- ● large towns
- • other towns

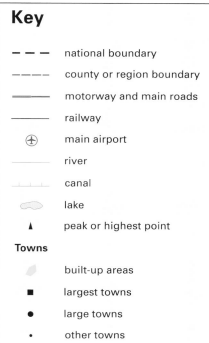

Land height

measured above sea level

- more than 1000m
- 500-1000m
- 200-500m
- 100-200m
- less than 100m

Dublin
Manchester
Liverpool
Birmingham
Cardiff

Transverse Mercator Projection
© Oxford University Press

Scale

10 km

One centimetre on the map measures 10 kilometres on the ground.

1 cm

0   10   20   30   40 km

Transverse Mercator Projection
© Oxford University Press

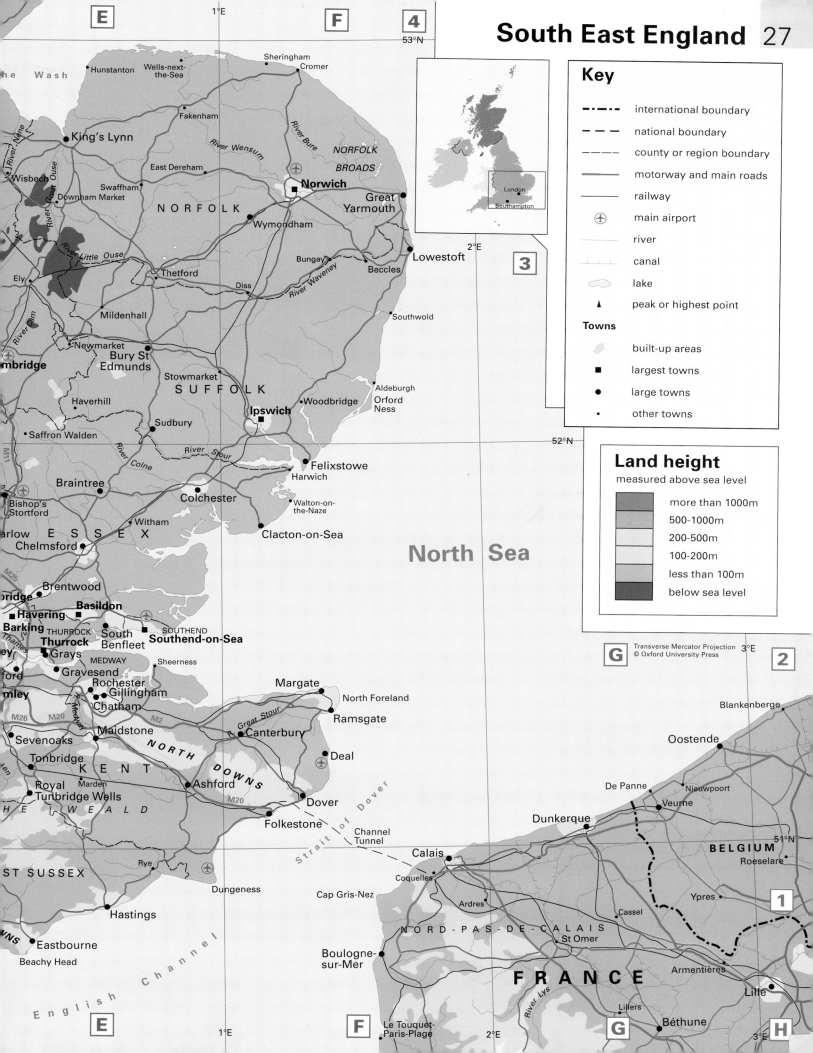

Key

- –·–·–· international boundary
- – – – national boundary
- – – – county or region boundary
- ——— motorway and main roads
- ——— railway
- ⊕ main airport
- —— river
- —||— canal
- ◌ lake
- ▲ peak or highest point

Towns

- built-up areas
- ■ largest towns
- ● large towns
- · other towns

Land height
measured above sea level

- more than 1000m
- 500-1000m
- 200-500m
- 100-200m
- less than 100m
- below sea level

Transverse Mercator Projection
© Oxford University Press

Map labels:

The Wash · Hunstanton · Wells-next-the-Sea · Sheringham · Cromer · Fakenham · King's Lynn · River Nene · River Wensum · River Bure · NORFOLK BROADS · East Dereham · Norwich · Swaffham · Downham Market · NORFOLK · Wymondham · Great Yarmouth · Wisbech · River Great Ouse · River Little Ouse · Ely · Thetford · Diss · River Waveney · Bungay · Beccles · Lowestoft · River Cam · Mildenhall · Southwold · Newmarket · Bury St Edmunds · mbridge · Stowmarket · SUFFOLK · Aldeburgh · Orford Ness · Haverhill · Ipswich · Woodbridge · Sudbury · Saffron Walden · River Colne · River Stour · Felixstowe · Harwich · Braintree · Bishop's Stortford · Colchester · Walton-on-the-Naze · arlow · ESSEX · Witham · Chelmsford · Clacton-on-Sea · M11 · Brentwood · North Sea · bridge · Havering · Basildon · Barking · THURROCK · South Benfleet · SOUTHEND · Southend-on-Sea · Thurrock · Grays · MEDWAY · Sheerness · ey · Gravesend · Rochester · Margate · ford · Gillingham · Chatham · North Foreland · mley · Great Stour · Ramsgate · Sevenoaks · Maidstone · Canterbury · Tonbridge · NORTH DOWNS · Deal · KENT · Marden · Royal Tunbridge Wells · Ashford · M20 · Dover · HE WEAL D · Folkestone · Channel Tunnel · ST SUSSEX · Rye · Strait of Dover · Dungeness · Calais · Cap Gris-Nez · Coquelles · Hastings · Ardres · NORD-PAS-DE-CALAIS · Eastbourne · Beachy Head · Boulogne-sur-Mer · FRANCE · River Lys · St Omer · Cassel · Lillers · Le Touquet-Paris-Plage · Béthune · Armentières · Lille · Blankenberge · Oostende · De Panne · Nieuwpoort · Veurne · Dunkerque · BELGIUM · Roeselare · Ypres · English Channel · North Sea · 52°N · 51°N

Scale

10 km

One centimetre on the map measures 10 kilometres on the ground.

1 cm

0   10   20   30   40 km

Key

–··–··–	international boundary
– – –	national boundary
–·–·–	county or region boundary
▬▬▬	motorway and main roads
———	railway
⊕	main airport
——	river
‡	canal
⬯	lake
▲	peak or highest point

Towns

⬭	built-up areas
■	largest towns
●	large towns
·	other towns

Land height

measured above sea level

	more than 1000m
	500–1000m
	200–500m
	100–200m
	less than 100m

Transverse Mercator Projection
© Oxford University Press

ATLANTIC OCEAN

Bristol Channel

Lundy

Ilfracombe   Lynton   Minehead
                                Dunkery Be
                                ▲ 519m
                    Braunton   River Exe
Bideford Bay   Barnstaple   EXMOOR
                                    South
Hartland   Molton
Point   Bideford   River Taw

           Great
           Torrington   Tiverton
    River Torridge
                    D E V O N   Cullor
Bude   Bude
Bay   Holsworthy   Crediton
                    Hatherleigh

Boscastle   Okehampton   River   Exeter
                                    Yes Tor   Exm
            Launceston   619   DARTMOOR
Trevose Head   Brown Willy   R. Teign   Dawlis
        Padstow   ▲ 420m   Bovey Tracey Teignmouth
    Wadebridge BODMIN   R. Tavy Newton Abbot
              MOOR   R. Tamar Tavistock
Newquay   Bodmin   River Fowey   Buckfastleigh   Tor
        CORNWALL   Liskeard   R. Dart   TORBAY
                    Lostwithiel   PLYMOUTH   Totnes   Brix
St Agnes   River Fal St   Fowey Saltash
        Redruth   Austell   Torpoint Plymouth   Dartmouth
Truro   Looe   Kingsbridge
St Ives Camborne   Bigbury Salcombe Start
    Penryn   Bay   Bay
St Just Falmouth   Start Poir
Penzance Helston
Sennen
Land's   Mullion
End   Mount's Bay

Bryher   St Martin's
Tresco
    St Mary's
    Hugh Town
Isles of
Scilly   Lizard Lizard
                    Point

ATLANTIC
OCEAN

D Cardiff 3°W
Clevedon
Barry
Weston-super-Mare
NORTH SOMERSET
BATH AND NORTH EAST SOMERSET
Keynsham
Bath
BRISTOL Bristol Kingswood E Chippenham 2°W
Calne
Devizes
Trowbridge
WILTSHIRE
Westbury SALISBURY PLAIN
Warminster
F 297m Walbury Hill
Basingstoke 1°W Camberley Farnborough G Woking Epsom SURREY
Aldershot Guildford
Andover Farnham Dorking

MENDIP HILLS
Wells
Shepton Mallet
Glastonbury
Frome
HAMPSHIRE DOWNS
Amesbury
River Test
Stockbridge
Alton
NORTH DOWNS
4

QUANTOCK HILLS
Bridgwater
dgwater Bay
Mere
Wincanton
Shaftesbury
Salisbury
R. Itchen
Winchester
HAMPSHIRE
Romsey
Petersfield
SOUTH DOWNS
Haslemere
Horsham
51°N
WEST SUSSEX

OMERSET
Taunton
Vellington
River Tone
M5
River Yeo
Ilchester
Yeovil
Sherborne
River Avon
Eastleigh
River Meon
Totton
Southampton
SOUTHAMPTON
M27
Waterlooville
Havant
Chichester
Arundel
Worthing

Ilminster
Crewkerne
Chard
River Axe
Axminster
loniton
River Parrett

Blandford Forum
Wimborne Minster
DORSET
Ringwood
Fawley
Fareham
Gosport
PORTSMOUTH
Portsmouth
Bognor Regis
Littlehampton

Bridport
River Stour
POOLE
Poole
BOURNEMOUTH
Christchurch
Lymington
Cowes
The Solent
Selsey Bill

Lyme Regis
Dorchester
River Frome
Wareham
Bournemouth
Newport
Ryde

Seaton
Sidmouth
Lyme Bay
Weymouth
Swanage
St Alban's Head
ISLE OF WIGHT
Sandown
Shanklin
3

The Needles
St Catherine's Point
Portland Bill

English Channel

50°N

Cap de la Hague
Auderville
Barfleur
Alderney
Cherbourg
Baie de la Seine
2

Valognes
Guernsey
St Peter-Port
Sark
FRANCE
CHANNEL ISLANDS
Carteret
Jersey
St Helier
Carentan
Isigny-sur-Mer
River Vire
Lessay
St-Lô

Coutainville
Coutances
River Orne
49°N
1

D 3°W E 2°W F 1°W G

Transverse Mercator Projection
© Oxford University Press

Most people in the United Kingdom live in large towns or cities.

Total number of people, 2001	
England	50 million
Scotland	5 million
Wales	3 million
N. Ireland	2 million
U.K.	**60 million**

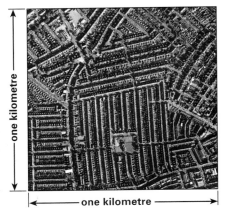

More than 250 people live in this square kilometre.

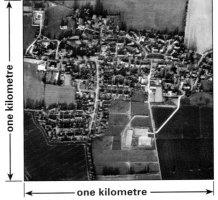

About 100 people live in this square kilometre.

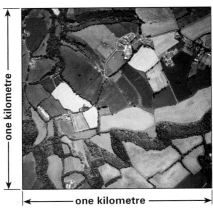

Fewer than 50 people live in this square kilometre.

Transverse Mercator Projection
© Oxford University Press

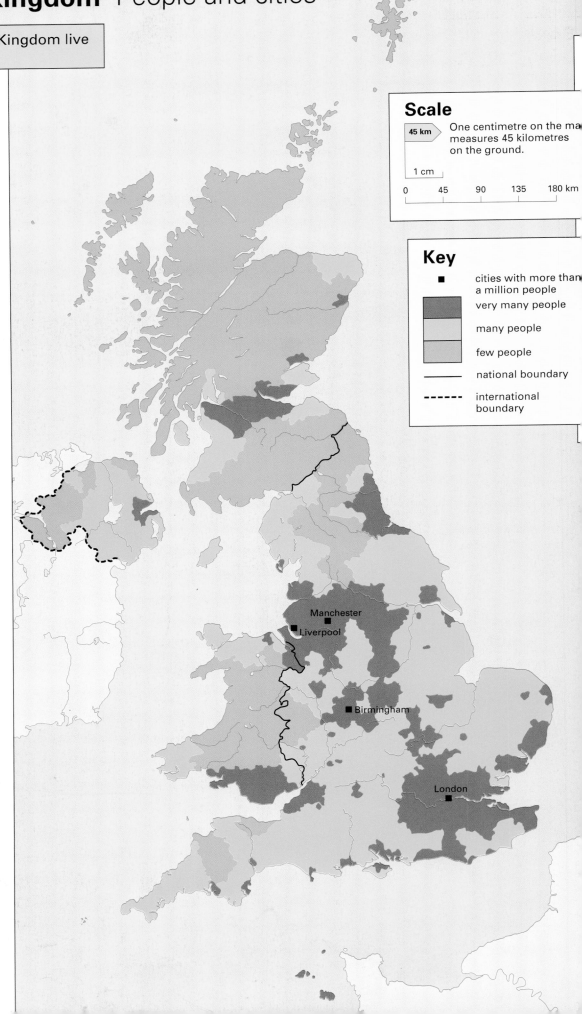

Scale

45 km ▸ One centimetre on the map measures 45 kilometres on the ground.

1 cm

| 0 | 45 | 90 | 135 | 180 km |

Key

■ cities with more than a million people

▓ very many people

▒ many people

░ few people

── national boundary

╌╌ international boundary

Manchester
Liverpool
■ Birmingham
London

The United Kingdom

Scale

45 km

One centimetre on the map measures 45 kilometres on the ground.

1 cm

| 0 | 45 | 90 | 135 | 180 km |

Farmers produce food by growing crops and keeping animals.

Key

	mostly livestock farms	cattle are kept for meat
	mostly hill farms	sheep are kept for meat and wool
	mostly dairy farms	cows are kept for milk
	mostly arable farms	crops are grown

Many farms in Britain are mixed farms. Farmers grow crops *and* keep animals.

🌲	forestry	trees are planted for wood
✳	market gardening	fruit and vegetables are grown
	no farming	built-up areas

More people work in offices
than in factories in the
United Kingdom.

Scale

45 km

One centimetre on the map
measures 45 kilometres
on the ground.

1 cm

0	45	90	135	180 km

Key

![major industrial area] major industrial area

• office and business centre

—— national boundary

------ international boundary

Jobs change

Over time some industries
close down.
People lose their jobs.

New industries are often
based on high technology
but not everyone can find work.

Central
Lowlands
Glasgow • • Edinburgh

City of
Belfast

Newcastle • • Tyneside

Leeds •
Greater
Manchester
West Yorkshire
Merseyside • Manchester
South Yorkshire

East
Midlands

West • Birmingham
Midlands

South
Wales
Cardiff • • Bristol

Greater
London
City of London
Croydon •

Southampton •

Coal, oil, and natural gas hold
energy which originally came
from the sun.

Scale

60 km

One centimetre on the map
measures 60 kilometres
on the ground.

1 cm

0	60	120	180	240 km

oil field
Claymore
Platform,
North Sea

Key

● largest coal mines

⊢╫⊣ gas field and pipeline

⊢╫⊣ oil field and pipeline

Largest power stations

▲ burning coal, oil or gas

▲ using water power

▲ using nuclear power

△ using wind power

wind generator
Blackmill Windfarm,
near Bridgend

Magnus

Tern
Statfjord
Brent
Ninian
North Alwyn

Foinaven

Bruce
Frigg
Beryl

Birch

Claymore
Piper
Scott

Shin

Conon
Kilmorack
Peterhead
Affric
Glenmoriston

Forties

Fulmar

Tummel
Cruachan
Breadalbane
Sloy

Longannet
Torness
Hunterston
Cockenzie

Windy
Standard

Ellington
Blyth Harbour

Owenreagh
Ballylumford

Hartlepool
Teesside

Heysham
Ravenspurn

South
Morecambe
Ferrybridge
Saltend
Coal
Clough
West Sole
Kellingley
Eggborough
Wylfa
Connah's
West Burton
Pickerill
Quay
Harworth
Cottam
Indefatigable
Dinorwig
Fiddler's
Thoresby
Hewett
Leman
Ferry
Ratcliffe-on-Soar
Mynydd
Cemaes
Rugeley
Penrhyddlan
Llidiart-y-waun
Daw Mill

Sizewell

Tower

Blackmill
Didcot
Barking
Tilbury
Aberthaw
Kingsnorth
Hinkley
Point
Dungeness
Delabole
Cold
Northcott
Carland Cross
Wytch
Farm

power station burning coal
Didcot Power Station,
Oxfordshire

Electricity is made in power stations
Thermal power stations
burn coal, oil, or gas to make
steam which drives turbines.
Nuclear power stations use the
heat from a nuclear reaction.
Hydro electric power stations use
water power.
Wind power stations use
wind generators.

Roads and railways do not always take the shortest route between places.

Scale

45 km ▷ One centimetre on the map measures 45 kilometres on the ground.

1 cm

0 45 90 135 180 km

Key

—— major road

—— motorway

—— main railway

• road or rail terminal

built-up areas

land over 200 metres

land below 200 metres

—— national boundary

valley of the River Taff near Cardiff, South Wales

bypass

Modern roads and motorways have gentle curves and often bypass towns to allow traffic to move at higher speeds. Rail networks avoid steep gradients.

Inverness

Aberdeen

Dundee

M90

M9

Glasgow M8

Edinburgh

M74

Coleraine

Londonderry

Larne

M2

Stranraer

Belfast

M1

Newcastle upon Tyne

A1(M)

Newry

Middlesbrough

M6

Kingston upon Hull

Leeds

M62

M180

A1(M)

Holyhead

Liverpool

Manchester

M1

M56

Sheffield

M6

Nottingham

M54

Norwich

Birmingham

Leicester

M5

M42

M6

M1

A1(M)

M11

Fishguard

M50

M40

M25

M4

Cardiff

Bristol

M4

London

M2

Dover

M3

M25

M23

M20

Folkestone

Channel Tunnel

Calais

Southampton

M27

Weymouth

M5

Penzance

F R A N C E

Transverse Mercator Projection
© Oxford University Press

Key

- —— country boundary
- ········ main United Kingdom airways
- ········ other airways
- ✈ major United Kingdom airport
- ✈ other major airport
- —— car ferry route
- • major car ferry port
- ⚑ major United Kingdom sea port
- built-up areas

Scale

90 km One centimetre on the map measures 90 kilometres on the ground.

1 cm

| 0 | 90 | 180 | 270 | 360 km |

Ports and airports link the United Kingdom with the rest of the world.

Airways are sky routes used by large transport jets. They are divided into layers so that aeroplanes can travel safely in opposite directions.

NORWAY
SWEDEN
to the Faeroe Islands
Sullom Voe
Lerwick
Bergen
Haugesund
Stavanger
Gothenburg
Aberdeen Dyce
Aberdeen
DENMARK
Forth
Glasgow
Edinburgh
Esbjerg
Copenhagen
Larne
Stranraer
Newcastle
Belfast
Belfast
Newcastle
Tees and Hartlepool
REPUBLIC OF IRELAND
UNITED KINGDOM
Dublin
Dún Laoghaire
Liverpool
Holyhead
Manchester
Grimsby
Hamburg
POLAND
Cork
Rosslare
East Midlands
Birmingham
Berlin
Fishguard
Milford Haven
Swansea
London Stansted
Felixstowe
NETHERLANDS
Amsterdam
London Luton
Harwich
Hook of Holland
Amsterdam Schiphol
GERMANY
London Heathrow
London
Southampton
London Gatwick
Dover
Zeebrugge
Ruhr
Plymouth
Portsmouth
Newhaven
Calais
Brussels
CZECH REPUBLIC
BELGIUM
Dieppe
LUXEMBOURG
Cherbourg
le Havre
Frankfurt
Jersey
Caen
Paris Charles de Gaulle
Roscoff
St- Malo
Paris Orly
Nantes
FRANCE
Santander
Bilbao
SPAIN

Damage to our land, sea, and air is called pollution.

Scale

45 km

One centimetre on the map measures 45 kilometres on the ground.

1 cm

| 0 | 45 | 90 | 135 | 180 km |

Key

built-up areas

most polluted rivers and estuaries

most polluted coasts and beaches

Areas affected by acid rain

heavy pollution

moderate pollution

light pollution

ATLANTIC OCEAN

North Sea

Loch Fyne

Firth of Forth

River Clyde

R. Tyne

R. Lagan

R. Bann

Irish Sea

R. Ribble

R. Aire

River Mersey

R. Don

R. Humber

River Trent

R. Nene

R. Avon

R. Severn

R. Thames

Bristol Channel

E n g l i s h   C h a n n e l

How to fight pollution

• Poisonous gases from cars and factories

• Poisonous waste in rivers from factories and farms

• Loud noise from aircraft, factories and traffic

• Dumping raw sewage in the sea

• Leaving litter

STOP

Tranverse Mercator Projection
© Oxford University Press

Protecting nature, resources, and buildings is called conservation.

Scale

45 km

One centimetre on the map measures 45 kilometres on the ground.

1 cm

0   45   90   135   180 km

Key

National Parks

areas of outstanding scenery and beauty

protected coast

★ World Heritage Sites

major built-up areas

National Park
Snowdonia

Area of outstanding scenery and beauty
Countryside in the Cotswolds

Protected coast
Pembrokeshire Coast

World Heritage Site
Stonehenge, Wiltshire

★ The Heart of Neolithic Orkney

★ St. Kilda

South Lewis, Harris and North Uist

Wester Ross

Cairngorms

Aberdeen

Ben Nevis and Glen Coe

Dundee

The Trossachs

Loch Lomond

Jura

Glasgow

★ Old and New Towns of Edinburgh

Edinburgh

New Lanark ★

Upper Tweeddale

Giant's Causeway ★

Antrim Coast and Glens

Sperrin Mountains

Belfast

Mourne Mountains

Northumberland

Hadrian's Wall ★

Newcastle upon Tyne

★ Durham Castle/ Cathedral

North Pennines

Middlesbrough

Lake District

Yorkshire Dales

North York Moors

Nidderdale

Forest of Bowland

★ Fountains Abbey/ Studley Royal Park

Saltaire ★

Leeds

Kingston upon Hull

Manchester

Liverpool

Sheffield

★ Liverpool- Maritime Mercantile City

Lincolnshire Wolds

Anglesey

Clwydian Range

Castles/Town Walls ★ of King Edward

Peak District

Llŷn

Snowdonia

Derwent ★ Valley Mills

Nottingham

Ironbridge Gorge ★

Shropshire Hills

Leicester

Birmingham

Norfolk Coast

Norwich

The Broads

The Broads

Pembrokeshire Coast

Wye Valley

Blenheim Palace ★

Suffolk Coast and Heaths

Brecon Beacons

Cotswolds

London

Blaenafon ★

Cardiff

Gower

Bristol

★ Bath

North Wessex Downs

Chilterns

Tower of London ★

Maritime Greenwich ★

Kew Gardens ★★★

Westminster Palace/Abbey

★ Canterbury Cathedral

Kent Downs

Stonehenge/ ★ Avebury

Exmoor

Cranbourne Chase

Surrey Hills

High Weald

Blackdown Hills

Dorset

New Forest

Southampton

South Downs

Bodmin Moor

Dartmoor

Dorset and ★ East Devon Coast

Isle of Wight

Transverse Mercator Projection
Oxford University Press

Europe is the smallest continent but is the most crowded.

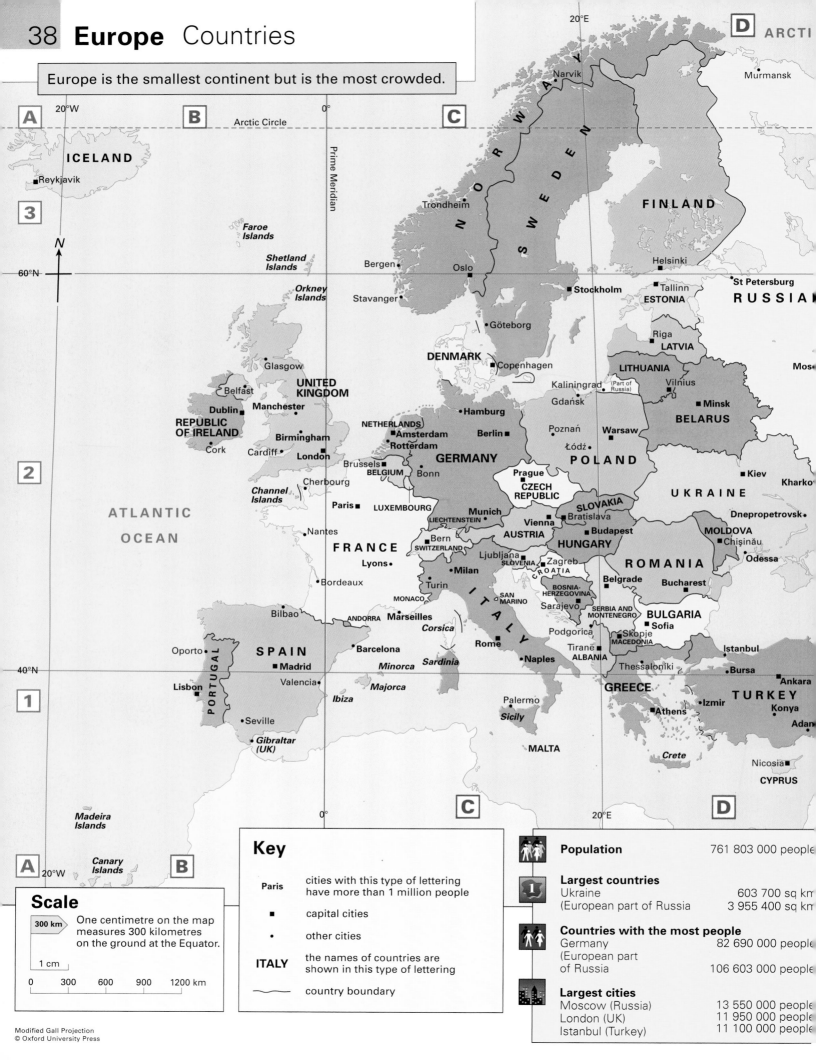

ARCTIC

A 20°W

B Arctic Circle

0°

C

D 20°E

Murmansk

Narvik

ICELAND

■ Reykjavik

3

Faroe Islands

Shetland Islands

60°N

N O R W A Y

Trondheim

S W E D E N

FINLAND

Bergen

Oslo

Helsinki

St Petersburg

Orkney Islands

Stavanger

Göteborg

■ Stockholm

■ Tallinn

ESTONIA

RUSSIA

Glasgow

Mose...

Belfast

UNITED KINGDOM

Manchester

Dublin ■

DENMARK

■ Copenhagen

Riga

LATVIA

LITHUANIA

Kaliningrad (Part of Russia)

Vilnius

■ Minsk

BELARUS

REPUBLIC OF IRELAND

Cork

Birmingham

Cardiff

London ●

NETHERLANDS

• Hamburg

Amsterdam

Berlin ■

Poznań

Gdańsk

■ Warsaw

● Kiev

Kharko...

Channel Islands

Cherbourg

Brussels

BELGIUM

Bonn

Rotterdam

GERMANY

POLAND

Łódź

UKRAINE

ATLANTIC

OCEAN

Paris ■

LUXEMBOURG

Prague

CZECH REPUBLIC

Munich

SLOVAKIA

Bratislava

Dnepropetrovsk •

Nantes

LIECHTENSTEIN

Vienna

Budapest ■

MOLDOVA

Chişinău ■

FRANCE

Bern

SWITZERLAND

AUSTRIA

HUNGARY

Odessa

Lyons

Ljubljana

Zagreb

SLOVENIA

C R O A T I A

ROMANIA

● Milan

Turin

BOSNIA-HERZEGOVINA

Belgrade ■

Bucharest ■

Bordeaux •

MONACO

SAN MARINO

Sarajevo

SERBIA AND MONTENEGRO

ANDORRA

Marseilles

Corsica

I T A L Y

Podgorica

BULGARIA

Sofia ●

Bilbao

Rome ■

Naples ●

Tiranë

ALBANIA

Skopje

MACEDONIA

Istanbul

Barcelona

Oporto

P O R T U G A L

SPAIN

■ Madrid

Minorca

Sardinia

Thessaloniki •

Bursa •

40°N

Ankara ■

1

Lisbon ■

Valencia •

Majorca

GREECE

TURKEY

Izmir •

Konya •

Seville •

Ibiza

Palermo •

Sicily

Athens ■

Adan...

Gibraltar (UK)

MALTA

Crete

Nicosia ■

CYPRUS

0°

C

20°E

D

Madeira Islands

A 20°W

Canary Islands

B

Scale

300 km ▷ One centimetre on the map measures 300 kilometres on the ground at the Equator.

1 cm

0   300   600   900   1200 km

Key

Paris — cities with this type of lettering have more than 1 million people

■ — capital cities

● — other cities

ITALY — the names of countries are shown in this type of lettering

— country boundary

Population 761 803 000 people

Largest countries
Ukraine 603 700 sq km
(European part of Russia 3 955 400 sq km

Countries with the most people
Germany 82 690 000 people
(European part of Russia 106 603 000 people

Largest cities
Moscow (Russia) 13 550 000 people
London (UK) 11 950 000 people
Istanbul (Turkey) 11 100 000 people

OCEAN

E   60°E   F

Arctic Circle

3

60°N

EDERATION   (RUSSIA)

• Perm

• Nizhniy
Novgorod

• Kazan

• Ufa

• Samara

2

Volgograd •

netsk

• Rostov-
on-Don

1

GEORGIA
Tbilisi ■

40°N

40°E

E

40°N

Modified Gall Projection
© Oxford University Press

The European Union

20°W   20°E   40°E

Arctic Circle

0°

60°N   60°N

Prime Meridian

40°N   40°N

20°W

20°E   40°E

The European Union

The European Union is a group of
countries which have agreed to
work together and share the same
plans for industry, agriculture,
transport, and trade.

Key

~~~ country boundary

countries which are
members of the
European Union

countries which have
applied to be members
of the European Union

other European countries

Scale   for both small maps

650 km   One centimetre on the map
measures 650 kilometres
on the ground at the Equator.

1 cm

0   650   1300   1950   2600 km

How big is Europe?

Arctic Circle

20°W   0°   20°E   40°E

Prime Meridian

See how long
journeys within
Europe take,
by air ✈ and
by rail 🚄

60°N

3.5 hours
London   Moscow
Berlin   35.5 hours
1 hour
Paris
15 hours   3.4 hours
Rome

40°N

Athens

20°W   0°   20°E   40°E

Europe is a continent of peninsulas and islands.

A 20°W

B 0° Arctic Circle

C

D 20°E ARCTI

A 20°W

B Strait of Gibraltar

Iceland

1491m ▲ Mount Hekla

3

N

60°N

Faroe Islands

Shetland Islands

Lofoten Islands

Kola Penins

SCANDINAVIAN HIGHLANDS

2470m ▲ Galdhøpiggen

R. Glomma

Gulf of Bothnia

Lake Ladoga

La Or

Orkney Islands

Outer Hebrides

Ben Nevis ▲1343m

North Sea

Lake Vänern

Lake Peipus

Gotland

Baltic Sea

Ireland

Great Britain

R. Thames

Bornholm

2

English Channel

Channel Islands

R. Seine

Friesian Islands

River Elbe

River Rhine

NORTH EUROPEAN PLAIN

River Vistula

Pripet Marshes

ATLANTIC OCEAN

River Loire

River Rhine

River Danube

CARPATHIANS

River Dniester

River Dnieper

Bay of Biscay

MASSIF CENTRAL

4810m Mont Blanc

ALPS

R. Rhône

River Po

APPENNINES

Adriatic Sea

River Danube

Black S

PYRENEES

River Ebro

River Duero

MESETA

Corsica

Sardinia

Tyrrhenian Sea

40°N

2917m ▲ Mount Olympus

ANATOLIA PLATEAU

1

River Tagus

Balearic Islands

Minorca

Majorca

Ibiza

Mediterranean

Sicily ▲3323m Mount Etna

Ionian Sea

Aegean Sea

Peloponnese

TAURU MOUNT

A 20°W

B Strait of Gibraltar

Malta

Sea

Crete

Cyprus

Prime Meridian

0°

C

D 20°E

Key

Colours show the height of the land.

- more than 2000 metres
- 1000 – 2000 metres
- 500 – 1000 metres
- 200 – 500 metres
- less than 200 metres
- this land is below the level of the sea
- ▲ peak or highest point
- river
- lake
- marsh
- ice cap

© Oxford University Press   Modified Gall Projection

Scale

➤ 300 km

One centimetre on the map measures 300 kilometres on the ground at the Equator.

1 cm

0   300   600   900   1200 km

Area		10 498 000 sq km
Highest peaks Mount Elbrus		5 642 m
Mont Blanc		4 810 m
Lowest point Caspian Sea		28 m below sea level
Largest freshwater lake Lake Ladoga		18 390 sq km
Longest river Volga		3 688 km

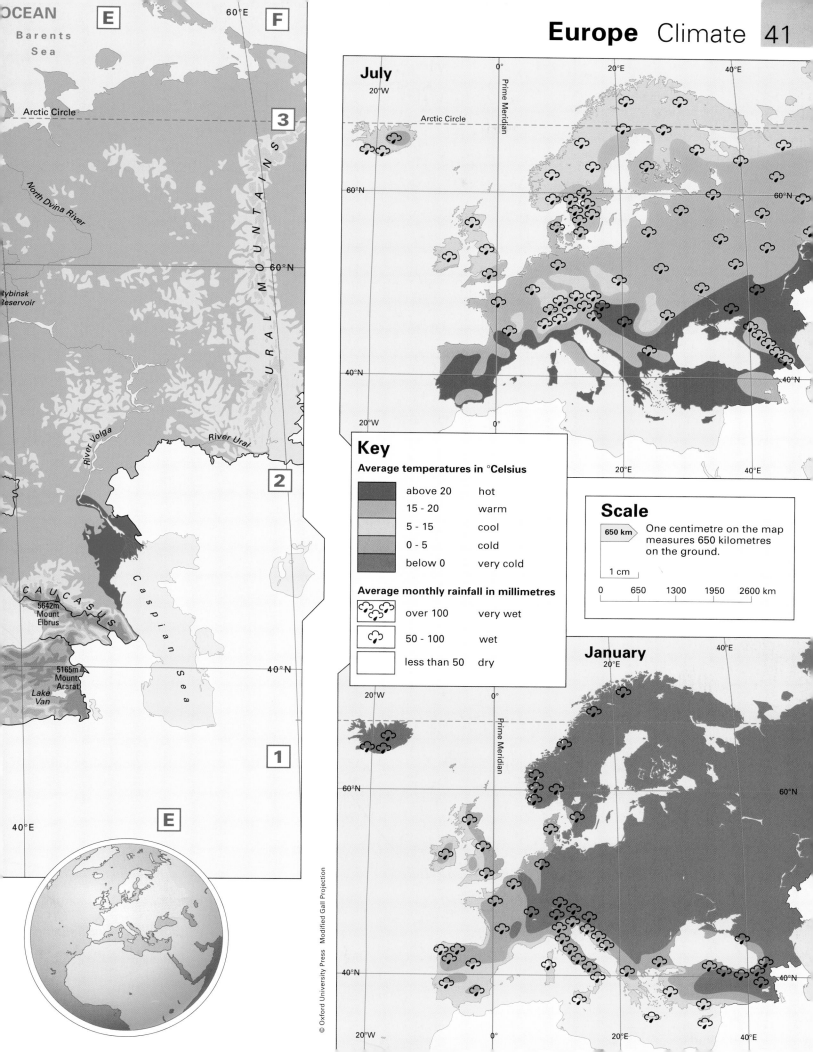

OCEAN

Barents
Sea

Arctic Circle

North Dvina River

Rybinsk
Reservoir

River Volga

River Ural

URAL MOUNTAINS

Caspian Sea

CAUCASUS
5642m Mount Elbrus

5165m Mount Ararat

Lake Van

© Oxford University Press   Modified Gall Projection

July

Arctic Circle

Prime Meridian

January

Prime Meridian

Key

Average temperatures in °Celsius

above 20	hot
15 - 20	warm
5 - 15	cool
0 - 5	cold
below 0	very cold

Average monthly rainfall in millimetres

over 100	very wet
50 - 100	wet
less than 50	dry

Scale

650 km

One centimetre on the map measures 650 kilometres on the ground.

1 cm

| 0 | 650 | 1300 | 1950 | 2600 km |

Of all the continents, Asia has the greatest variety of landscapes and people.

60°E · C · 80°E · D · 100°E · E · 120°E · F · 140°E

A · 40°E · B

Arctic Circle

6

60°N

RUSSIAN FEDERATION (RUSSIA)

· Yakutsk

St Petersburg

Moscow

Perm

Nizhniy Novgorod
Kazan
Ufa
Samara

Yekaterinburg
Chelyabinsk
Omsk
Novosibirsk

5

Astana

Volgograd
Rostov-on-Don
Gur'yev

KAZAKHSTAN

Ulan Bator
MONGOLIA

Harbin
Changchun · Jilin
Shenyang Fushun
Jinzhou Anshan
Yingkou Dandong
Beijing Dalian
Tianjin Pyongyang
Seoul
Qingdao
NORTH KOREA
SOUTH KOREA
Pusan

ARMENIA
Baku
Yerevan
AZERBAIJAN
UZBEKISTAN
Tashkent
Bishkek
KYRGYZSTAN
Almaty

TURKMENISTAN
Ashgabat
Dushanbe
TAJIKISTAN
Mashhad
Tabriz
Tehran
Esfahan

40°N

JAPAN
Nagoya Tokyo
Osaka Yokohama
Kita-Kyushu

Aleppo
Beirut
SYRIA Damascus
LEBANON
Amman
ISRAEL Jerusalem
JORDAN
Baghdad
IRAQ
Basra
IRAN
KUWAIT
Kuwait City
Busehr
BAHRAIN
QATAR
Doha
Abu Dhabi
Muscat

AFGHANISTAN
Kabul
Islamabad
Lahore
JAMMU AND KASHMIR
New Delhi
PAKISTAN

CHINA
Taiyuan
Lanzhou
Xi'an
Jinan
Zibo

Nanjing
Wuhan
Chengdu
Chongqing
Nanchang
Shanghai
Hangzhou
Wenzhou

4

Riyadh
SAUDI ARABIA
Jeddah
UNITED ARAB EMIRATES
OMAN

Karachi

NEPAL
Kathmandu
Kanpur
BHUTAN
Thimphu

Ahmadabad
BANGLADESH
Dhaka
Kolkata
Chittagong
MYANMAR

Taipei
TAIWAN
Kao-hsiung
Tropic of Cancer
Guangzhou
Hong Kong

San'a
YEMEN REPUBLIC

Mumbai
INDIA
Hyderabad

Hanoi
Vientiane
LAOS
VIETNAM
Yangon
THAILAND
Bangkok
CAMBODIA
Phnom Penh
Ho Chi Minh

Manila
Quezon City
PHILIPPINES

3

Bangalore
Chennai
SRI LANKA
Colombo

MALAYSIA
Bandar Seri Begawan
BRUNEI

MALDIVES

Medan
Kuala Lumpur
SINGAPORE

Equator

Palembang
INDONESIA

Jakarta
Semarang
Bandung
Surabaya
Dili
EAST TIMOR

2

INDIAN OCEAN

20°S

1

Tropic of Capricorn

Modified Gall Projection
© Oxford University Press

A · 40°E · B · 60°E · C · 80°E · D · 100°E · E · 120°E · F · 140°E

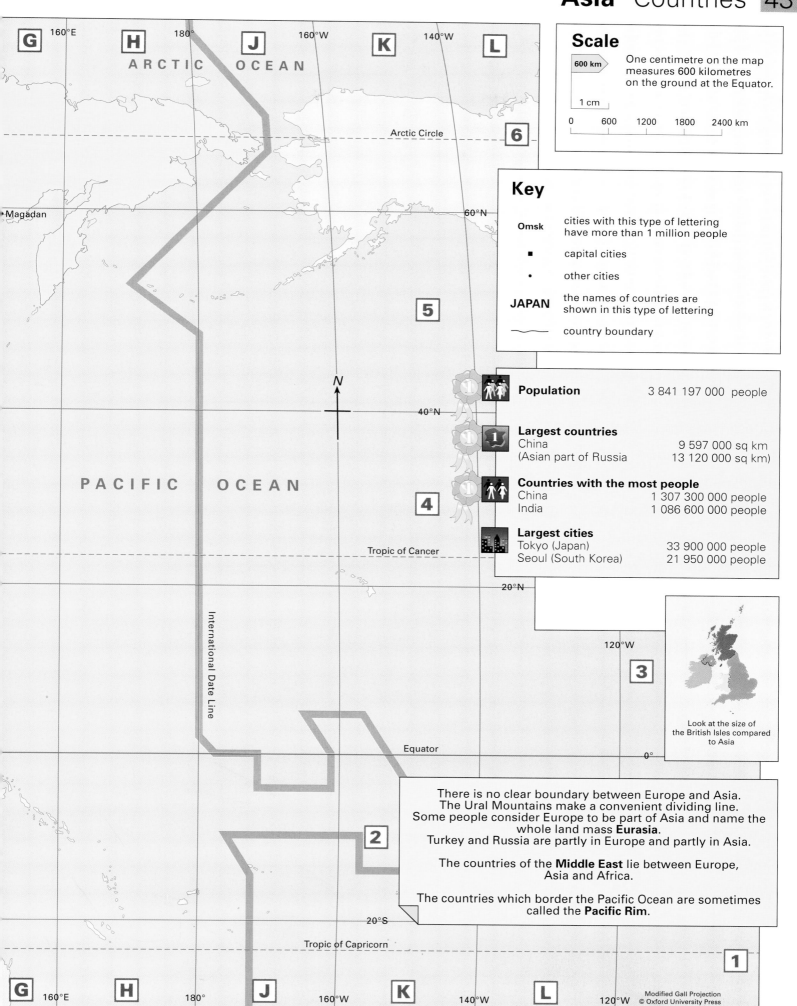

ARCTIC OCEAN

Arctic Circle

6

Magadan

60°N

5

PACIFIC OCEAN

N

40°N

4

Tropic of Cancer

20°N

International Date Line

120°W

3

Equator

0°

2

20°S

Tropic of Capricorn

1

Scale

600 km

One centimetre on the map measures 600 kilometres on the ground at the Equator.

1 cm

| 0 | 600 | 1200 | 1800 | 2400 km |

Key

Omsk — cities with this type of lettering have more than 1 million people

■ — capital cities

• — other cities

JAPAN — the names of countries are shown in this type of lettering

— country boundary

Population   3 841 197 000 people

Largest countries
China   9 597 000 sq km
(Asian part of Russia   13 120 000 sq km)

Countries with the most people
China   1 307 300 000 people
India   1 086 600 000 people

Largest cities
Tokyo (Japan)   33 900 000 people
Seoul (South Korea)   21 950 000 people

Look at the size of the British Isles compared to Asia

There is no clear boundary between Europe and Asia. The Ural Mountains make a convenient dividing line. Some people consider Europe to be part of Asia and name the whole land mass **Eurasia**. Turkey and Russia are partly in Europe and partly in Asia.

The countries of the **Middle East** lie between Europe, Asia and Africa.

The countries which border the Pacific Ocean are sometimes called the **Pacific Rim**.

Modified Gall Projection
© Oxford University Press

Asia covers one third of the land surface of the Earth.

Barents Sea

A **B** **C** **D** **E** **F**

20°E 40°E 60°E 80°E 100°E 120°E 140°E

CENTRAL SIBERIAN PLATEAU

Arctic Circle

SIBERIAN LOWLAND

Yenisey River

River Lena

Lake Onega

River Ob

Lake Ladoga

60°N

Angara River

Sea Okho

URAL MOUNTAINS

River Volga

River Irtysh

Lake Baykal

River Amur

5

ALTAI MOUNTAINS

Aral Sea

Lake Balkhash

Black Sea

CAUCASUS

5642m Mount Elbrus

Caspian Sea

Gobi Desert

Hokkaido

40°N

5165m Mount Ararat

7495m Communism Peak

KUNLUN SHAN

Hwang-Ho River

Sea of Japan

Mount Demavend △5671m

Korean Peninsula

Honshu

△Mount Fuji 3776m

HINDU KUSH

8611m K2

TIBETAN PLATEAU

Yellow Sea

Shikoku

R. Euphrates

R. Tigris

ZAGROS MOUNTAINS

River Indus

Red Basin

Kyushu

4

Dead Sea 395m below sea level

The Gulf

HIMALAYAS

Mount Everest △8848m

Yangtze River

East China Sea

Ryukyu Islands

Red Sea

Thar Desert

River Ganges

Brahmaputra R.

Irrawaddy River

Tropic of Cancer

20°N

△Mount Nabi Shu'ayb 3760m

Arabian Sea

WESTERN GHATS

DECCAN

Mouths of the Ganges

Salween River

South China Sea

Luzon

Socotra

Bay of Bengal

Mekong River

Mindoro

Andaman Islands

Gulf of Thailand

3

Andaman Sea

Mount Kinabalu 4101m△

Mindanao

Nicobar Islands

Malay Peninsula

Maldive Archipelago

Borneo

0° Equator

Sulawesi

Java Sea

New Guinea

5030m △ Jaya Peak

Sumatra

2

INDIAN OCEAN

Java

Bali

Arafura Sea

Timor Sea

20°S

1

Tropic of Capricorn

A **B** **C** **D** **E** **F**

40°E 60°E 80°E 100°E 120°E 140°E

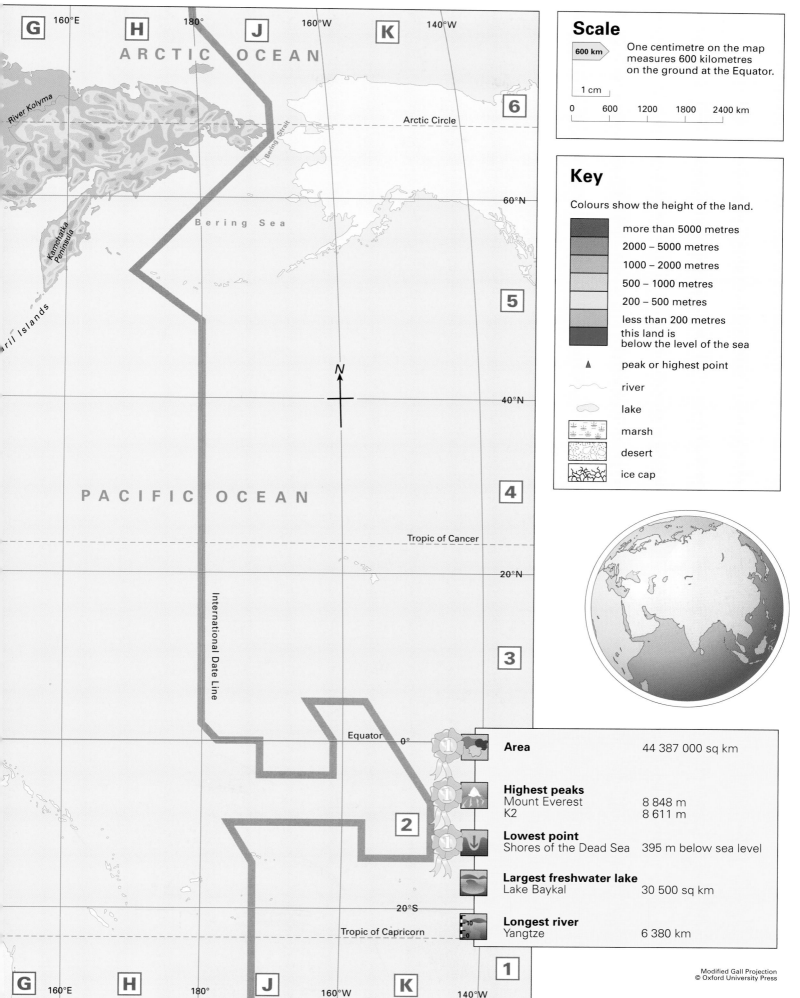

Scale

600 km

One centimetre on the map measures 600 kilometres on the ground at the Equator.

1 cm

| 0 | 600 | 1200 | 1800 | 2400 km |

Key

Colours show the height of the land.

more than 5000 metres
2000 – 5000 metres
1000 – 2000 metres
500 – 1000 metres
200 – 500 metres
less than 200 metres
this land is
below the level of the sea

▲ peak or highest point

river

lake

marsh

desert

ice cap

| **Area** | 44 387 000 sq km |

Highest peaks	
Mount Everest	8 848 m
K2	8 611 m

| **Lowest point** | |
| Shores of the Dead Sea | 395 m below sea level |

| **Largest freshwater lake** | |
| Lake Baykal | 30 500 sq km |

| **Longest river** | |
| Yangtze | 6 380 km |

Modified Gall Projection
© Oxford University Press

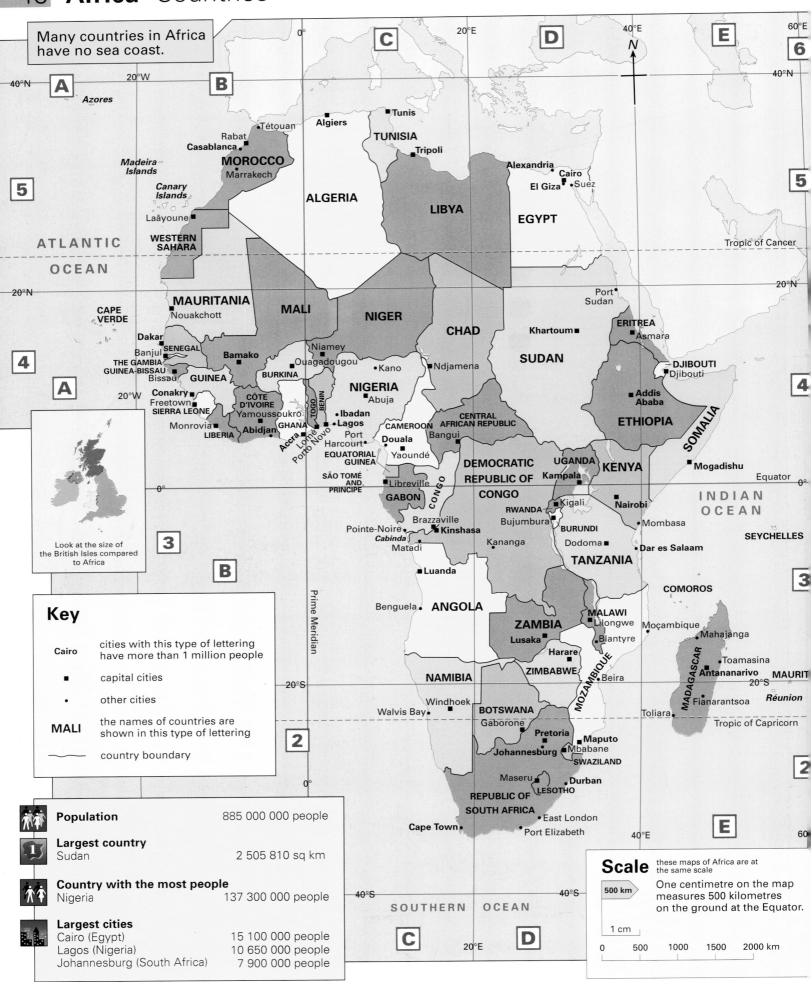

Many countries in Africa have no sea coast.

Key

Cairo — cities with this type of lettering have more than 1 million people

■ capital cities

• other cities

MALI — the names of countries are shown in this type of lettering

〰 country boundary

Look at the size of the British Isles compared to Africa

Population 885 000 000 people

Largest country
Sudan 2 505 810 sq km

Country with the most people
Nigeria 137 300 000 people

Largest cities
Cairo (Egypt) 15 100 000 people
Lagos (Nigeria) 10 650 000 people
Johannesburg (South Africa) 7 900 000 people

Scale these maps of Africa are at the same scale

500 km

One centimetre on the map measures 500 kilometres on the ground at the Equator.

1 cm

0   500   1000   1500   2000 km

Modified Gall Projection
© Oxford University Press

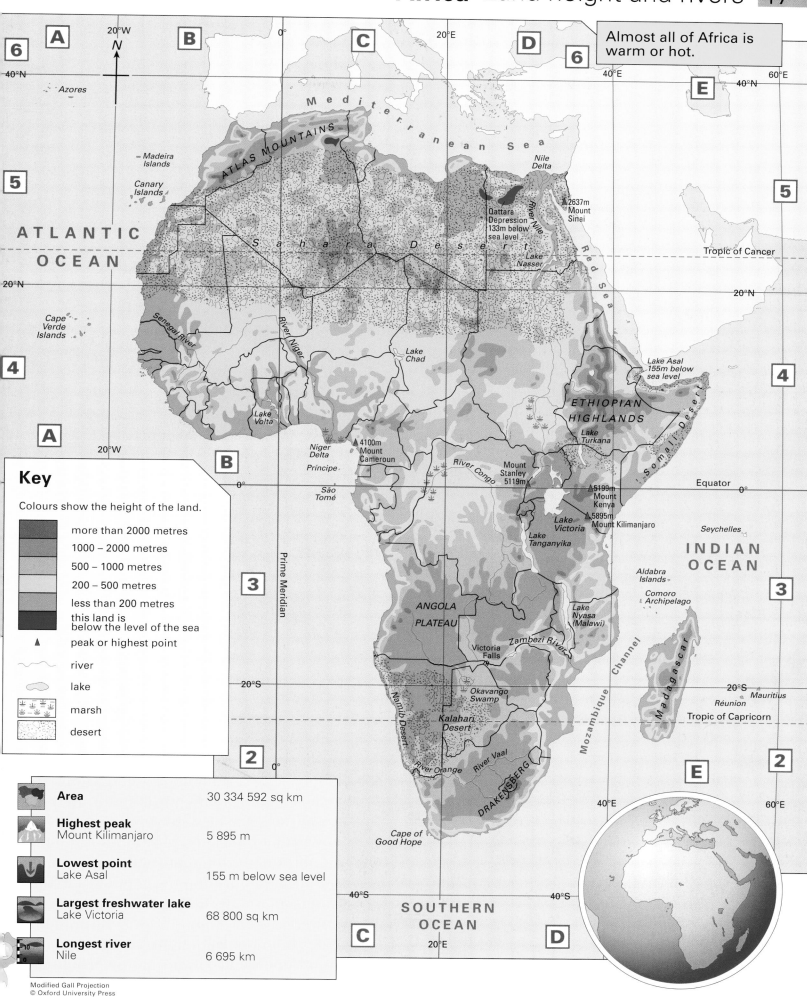

Almost all of Africa is warm or hot.

Key

Colours show the height of the land.

more than 2000 metres
1000 – 2000 metres
500 – 1000 metres
200 – 500 metres
less than 200 metres
this land is below the level of the sea
▲ peak or highest point
river
lake
marsh
desert

	Area	30 334 592 sq km
	Highest peak Mount Kilimanjaro	5 895 m
	Lowest point Lake Asal	155 m below sea level
	Largest freshwater lake Lake Victoria	68 800 sq km
	Longest river Nile	6 695 km

Modified Gall Projection
© Oxford University Press

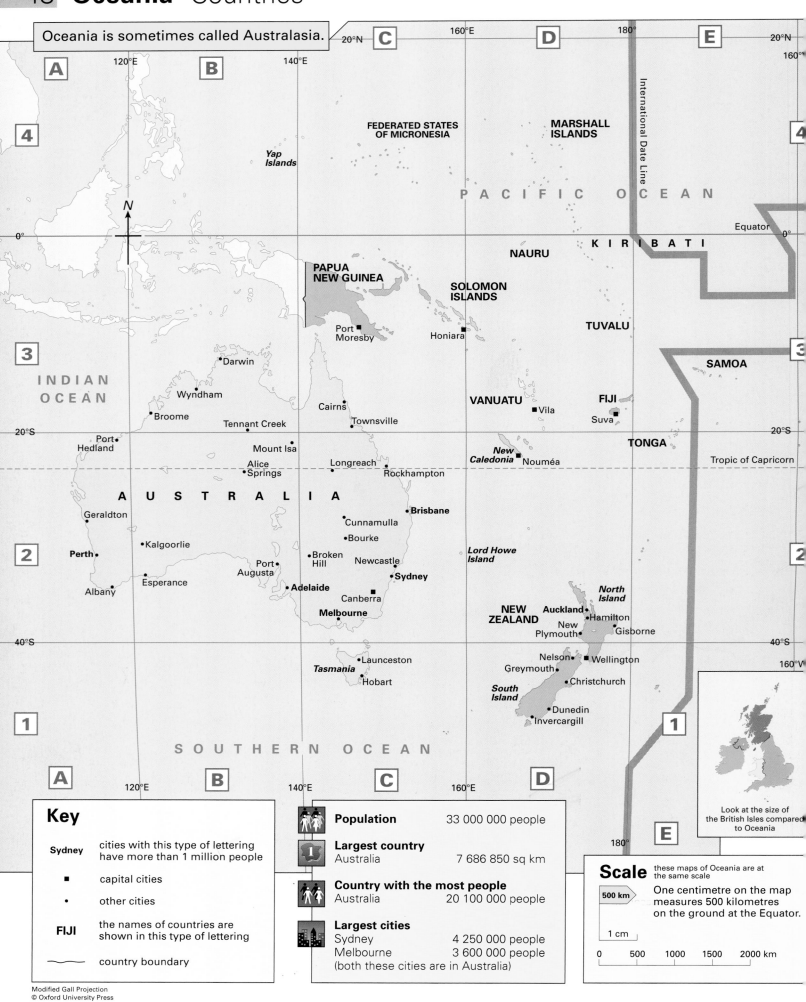

Oceania is sometimes called Australasia.

FEDERATED STATES OF MICRONESIA

MARSHALL ISLANDS

International Date Line

Yap Islands

PACIFIC OCEAN

Equator

KIRIBATI

NAURU

PAPUA NEW GUINEA

Port Moresby

SOLOMON ISLANDS

Honiara

TUVALU

INDIAN OCEAN

SAMOA

Darwin

Wyndham

Cairns

Townsville

VANUATU

Vila

FIJI

Suva

Broome

Tennant Creek

TONGA

Port Hedland

Mount Isa

Longreach

Rockhampton

New Caledonia

Nouméa

Tropic of Capricorn

Alice Springs

A U S T R A L I A

Geraldton

Cunnamulla

Brisbane

Lord Howe Island

Kalgoorlie

Bourke

Perth

Broken Hill

Newcastle

Port Augusta

Sydney

North Island

NEW ZEALAND

Auckland

Albany

Esperance

Adelaide

Canberra

Hamilton

New Plymouth

Gisborne

Melbourne

Launceston

Tasmania

Hobart

Nelson

Greymouth

Wellington

South Island

Christchurch

Dunedin

Invercargill

S O U T H E R N   O C E A N

Look at the size of the British Isles compared to Oceania

Key

Sydney — cities with this type of lettering have more than 1 million people

■ capital cities

• other cities

FIJI — the names of countries are shown in this type of lettering

⌒ country boundary

Population — 33 000 000 people

Largest country
Australia — 7 686 850 sq km

Country with the most people
Australia — 20 100 000 people

Largest cities
Sydney — 4 250 000 people
Melbourne — 3 600 000 people
(both these cities are in Australia)

Scale — these maps of Oceania are at the same scale

500 km

One centimetre on the map measures 500 kilometres on the ground at the Equator.

1 cm

0   500   1000   1500   2000 km

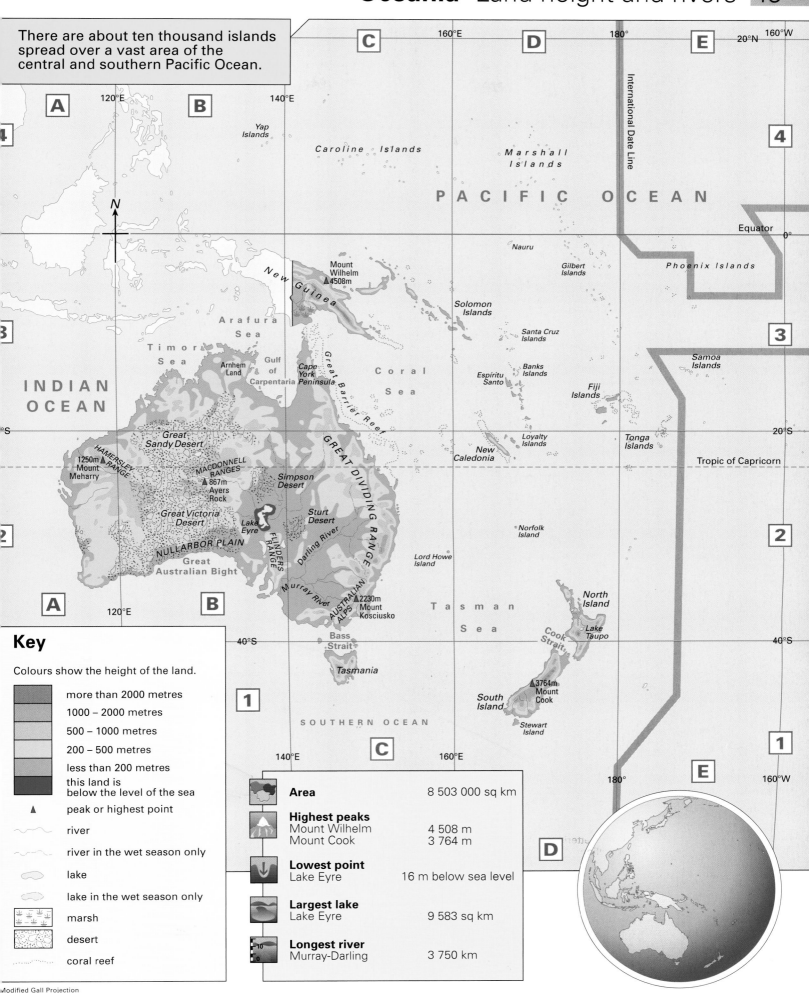

There are about ten thousand islands spread over a vast area of the central and southern Pacific Ocean.

160°E C D 180° E 20°N 160°W

120°E A B 140°E

Yap Islands

Caroline Islands

Marshall Islands

PACIFIC OCEAN

4

N

Equator 0°

Nauru

Gilbert Islands

Phoenix Islands

New Guinea

Mount Wilhelm ▲4508m

Solomon Islands

Arafura Sea

Timor Sea

Santa Cruz Islands

Coral Sea

3

Gulf of Carpentaria

Arnhem Land

Cape York Peninsula

Banks Islands

Samoa Islands

Espíritu Santo

INDIAN OCEAN

Great Barrier Reef

Fiji Islands

20°S

Great Sandy Desert

HAMERSLEY RANGE

1250m ▲ Mount Meharry

MACDONNELL RANGES

Simpson Desert

GREAT DIVIDING RANGE

Loyalty Islands

New Caledonia

Tonga Islands

Tropic of Capricorn

▲867m Ayers Rock

Great Victoria Desert

Lake Eyre

Sturt Desert

FLINDERS RANGE

Norfolk Island

2

NULLARBOR PLAIN

Darling River

Great Australian Bight

Lord Howe Island

Murray River

AUSTRALIAN ALPS

▲2230m Mount Kosciusko

Tasman Sea

North Island

Lake Taupo

Cook Strait

A 120°E B

Bass Strait

40°S

Tasmania

South Island

▲3764m Mount Cook

Stewart Island

1

SOUTHERN OCEAN

140°E C 160°E

180° E 160°W

Key

Colours show the height of the land.

	more than 2000 metres
	1000 – 2000 metres
	500 – 1000 metres
	200 – 500 metres
	less than 200 metres
	this land is below the level of the sea
▲	peak or highest point
～	river
～	river in the wet season only
◯	lake
◯	lake in the wet season only
〷	marsh
▦	desert
⋯	coral reef

	Area	8 503 000 sq km
	Highest peaks Mount Wilhelm Mount Cook	4 508 m 3 764 m
	Lowest point Lake Eyre	16 m below sea level
	Largest lake Lake Eyre	9 583 sq km
	Longest river Murray-Darling	3 750 km

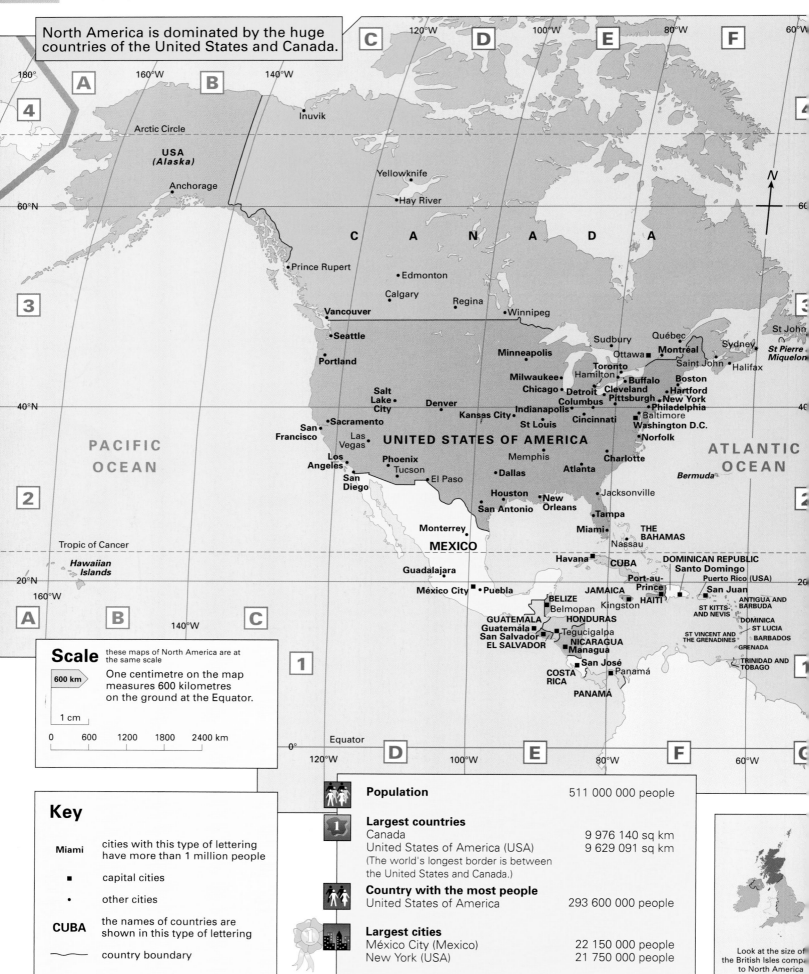

North America is dominated by the huge countries of the United States and Canada.

Arctic Circle

Inuvik

USA (Alaska)

Anchorage

Yellowknife

Hay River

C A N A D A

Prince Rupert

Edmonton

Calgary

Regina

Winnipeg

Vancouver

Seattle

Sudbury

Québec

Sydney

St John

St Pierre Miquelon

Minneapolis

Ottawa

Montréal

Saint John

Halifax

Portland

Milwaukee

Hamilton

Toronto

Buffalo

Boston

Chicago

Detroit

Cleveland

Hartford

Salt Lake City

Denver

Columbus

Pittsburgh

New York

Kansas City

Indianapolis

St Louis

Cincinnati

Philadelphia

Baltimore

San Francisco

Sacramento

UNITED STATES OF AMERICA

Washington D.C.

Norfolk

PACIFIC OCEAN

Las Vegas

Memphis

Charlotte

ATLANTIC OCEAN

Los Angeles

Phoenix

Tucson

Dallas

Atlanta

San Diego

El Paso

Bermuda

Jacksonville

Houston

New Orleans

San Antonio

Tampa

Monterrey

Miami

THE BAHAMAS

MEXICO

Nassau

Tropic of Cancer

Hawaiian Islands

Havana

CUBA

DOMINICAN REPUBLIC

Santo Domingo

Guadalajara

Puerto Rico (USA)

México City

Puebla

Port-au-Prince

San Juan

JAMAICA

ANTIGUA AND BARBUDA

BELIZE

HAITI

Belmopan

Kingston

ST KITTS-AND NEVIS

GUATEMALA

HONDURAS

DOMINICA

Guatemála

Tegucigalpa

ST LUCIA

San Salvador

NICARAGUA

ST VINCENT AND THE GRENADINES

BARBADOS

EL SALVADOR

Managua

GRENADA

San José

Panamá

TRINIDAD AND TOBAGO

COSTA RICA

PANAMÁ

Scale

these maps of North America are at the same scale

600 km

One centimetre on the map measures 600 kilometres on the ground at the Equator.

1 cm

0 600 1200 1800 2400 km

Equator

Key

Miami — cities with this type of lettering have more than 1 million people

■ — capital cities

• — other cities

CUBA — the names of countries are shown in this type of lettering

— country boundary

Population — 511 000 000 people

Largest countries
Canada — 9 976 140 sq km
United States of America (USA) — 9 629 091 sq km
(The world's longest border is between the United States and Canada.)

Country with the most people
United States of America — 293 600 000 people

Largest cities
México City (Mexico) — 22 150 000 people
New York (USA) — 21 750 000 people

Look at the size of the British Isles compared to North America

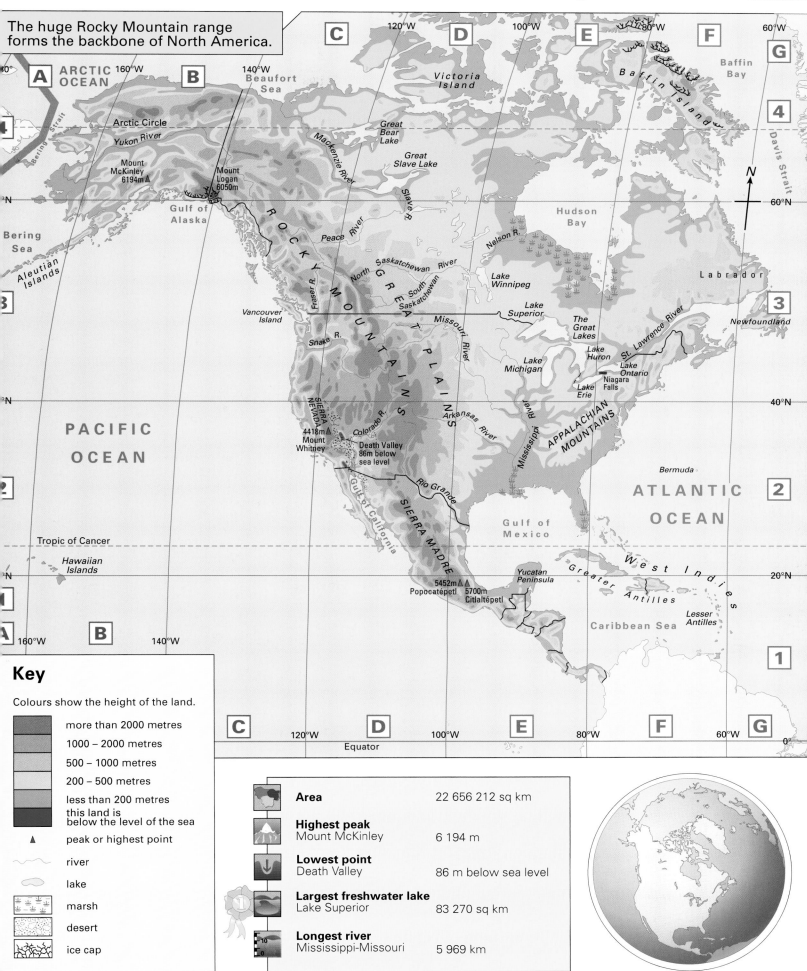

The huge Rocky Mountain range forms the backbone of North America.

Key

Colours show the height of the land.

more than 2000 metres
1000 – 2000 metres
500 – 1000 metres
200 – 500 metres
less than 200 metres
this land is below the level of the sea

▲ peak or highest point
river
lake
marsh
desert
ice cap

Area	22 656 212 sq km	
Highest peak Mount McKinley	6 194 m	
Lowest point Death Valley	86 m below sea level	
Largest freshwater lake Lake Superior	83 270 sq km	
Longest river Mississippi-Missouri	5 969 km	

Modified Gall Projection
© Oxford University Press

ARCTIC OCEAN
Bering Strait
Beaufort Sea
Victoria Island
Baffin Bay
Baffin Island
Arctic Circle
Yukon River
Mount McKinley 6194m ▲
Mount Logan 6050m
Gulf of Alaska
Mackenzie River
Great Bear Lake
Great Slave Lake
Hudson Bay
Davis Strait
Bering Sea
Aleutian Islands
Peace River
Slave R.
Nelson R.
Labrador
North Saskatchewan River
South Saskatchewan River
Lake Winnipeg
Fraser R.
ROCKY MOUNTAINS
GREAT PLAINS
Vancouver Island
Snake R.
Missouri River
Lake Superior
The Great Lakes
Newfoundland
St. Lawrence River
Lake Huron
Lake Michigan
Lake Ontario
Niagara Falls
Lake Erie
SIERRA NEVADA
4418m ▲ Mount Whitney
Death Valley 86m below sea level
Arkansas River
Mississippi River
APPALACHIAN MOUNTAINS
PACIFIC OCEAN
Bermuda
Colorado R.
Rio Grande
ATLANTIC OCEAN
Gulf of California
SIERRA MADRE
Gulf of Mexico
Tropic of Cancer
Hawaiian Islands
Yucatan Peninsula
Greater Antilles
West Indies
5452m ▲▲ Popocatépetl 5700m Citlaltépetl
Lesser Antilles
Caribbean Sea
Equator

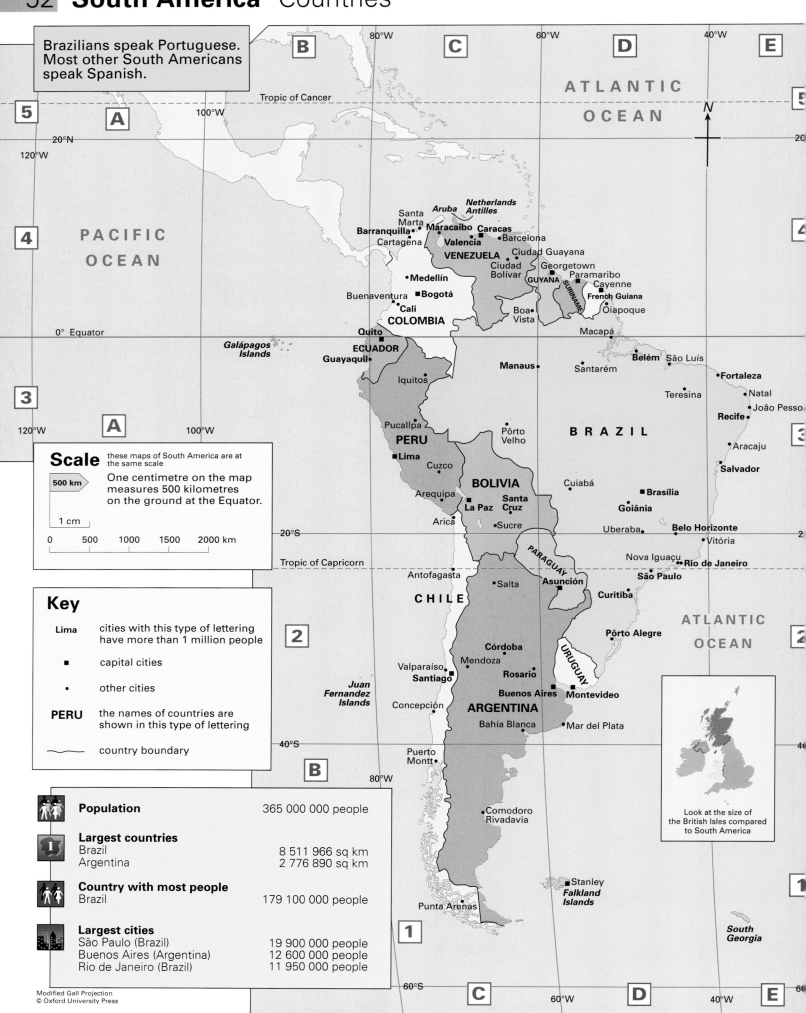

Brazilians speak Portuguese. Most other South Americans speak Spanish.

5

A

Tropic of Cancer

20°N

120°W

4

PACIFIC
OCEAN

100°W

0° Equator

3

120°W

100°W

A

Scale

these maps of South America are at the same scale

500 km

One centimetre on the map measures 500 kilometres on the ground at the Equator.

1 cm

0   500   1000   1500   2000 km

Key

Lima   cities with this type of lettering have more than 1 million people

■   capital cities

•   other cities

PERU   the names of countries are shown in this type of lettering

⌒   country boundary

B

80°W

B   **C**   60°W   **D**   40°W   **E**

ATLANTIC

OCEAN

N

5

20°

4

Santa
Marta
Aruba *Netherlands
Antilles*
Barranquilla **Maracaibo** **Caracas**
Cartagena **Valencia** Barcelona
VENEZUELA Ciudad Guayana
Ciudad **Georgetown**
Medellín Bolívar Paramaribo
Buenaventura **Bogotá** **GUYANA** Cayenne
Cali Boa **French Guiana**
COLOMBIA Vista Oiapoque
Quito Macapá
ECUADOR
Guayaquil Belém São Luís **Fortaleza**
Manaus Santarém Teresina Natal
Iquitos João Pesso
B R A Z I L **Recife**
Pucallpa Pôrto Aracaju
PERU Velho **Salvador**
Lima Cuzco
BOLIVIA Cuiabá **Brasília**
Arequipa **Santa** Goiânia
La Paz **Cruz**
Arica •Sucre Uberaba **Belo Horizonte**
Vitória
20°S
Tropic of Capricorn PARAGUAY Nova Iguaçu
Antofagasta •Salta **Asunción** **Rio de Janeiro**
São Paulo
C H I L E **Curitiba**
2
Córdoba **Pôrto Alegre**
Mendoza URUGUAY
Valparaíso **Rosario**
Juan **Santiago** **Buenos Aires** Montevideo
Fernandez **ARGENTINA**
Islands Concepción
Bahía Blanca •Mar del Plata
40°S

B

80°W

Puerto
Montt

•Comodoro
Rivadavia

Punta Arenas

1

60°S

C   60°W   **D**   40°W   **E**

ATLANTIC

OCEAN

2

■Stanley
*Falkland
Islands*

1

*South
Georgia*

Look at the size of the British Isles compared to South America

👪	**Population**	365 000 000 people
🗺	**Largest countries** Brazil Argentina	8 511 966 sq km 2 776 890 sq km
👫	**Country with most people** Brazil	179 100 000 people
🏙	**Largest cities** São Paulo (Brazil) Buenos Aires (Argentina) Rio de Janeiro (Brazil)	19 900 000 people 12 600 000 people 11 950 000 people

The Amazon rainforest contains half of all known plants and animals in the world.

PACIFIC OCEAN

Tropic of Cancer

ATLANTIC OCEAN

Equator

PACIFIC OCEAN

Tropic of Capricorn

ATLANTIC OCEAN

SOUTHERN OCEAN

Lake Maracaibo

River Orinoco

Angel Falls

GUIANA HIGHLANDS

ANDES

Llanos

Cotopaxi △5897m

6310m Chimborazo

Galápagos Islands

Selvas

River Amazon

River Madeira

River Tocantins

BRAZILIAN HIGHLANDS

São Francisco

Lake Titicaca

Atacama Desert

ANDES

Mato Grosso

GRAN CHACO

Paraguay River

River Paraná

BRAZIL PLATEAU

△6908m Ojos del Salado

△6960m Aconcagua

Juan Fernandez Islands

River Paraná

River Plate

Pampa

Valdés Peninsula

R. Chubut

Patagonia

Falkland Islands

Tierra del Fuego

South Georgia

Cape Horn

N

Key

Colours show the height of the land.

- more than 5000 metres
- 2000 – 5000 metres
- 1000 – 2000 metres
- 500 – 1000 metres
- 200 – 500 metres
- less than 200 metres
- this land is below the level of the sea
- ▲ peak or highest point
- river
- lake
- marsh
- desert
- ice cap

Area		17 832 000 sq km
Highest peaks		
Mount Aconcagua		6 960 m
Ojos del Salado		6 908 m
Lowest point		
Valdés Peninsula		40 m below sea level
Largest freshwater lake		
Lake Titicaca		8 340 sq km
Longest river		
Amazon		6 516 km
World's highest waterfall		
Angel Falls (Venezuela)		979 m

Modified Gall Projection
© Oxford University Press

Antarctica has 90% of all of the ice in the world.

Scale

| 340 km | One centimetre on the map measures 340 kilometres on the ground. |

1 cm

| 0 | 340 | 680 | 1020 | 1360 km |

Area 13 340 000 sq km

Highest point
Vinson Massif 5 140 m

World's longest glacier
Lambert Glacier 400 km

Look at the size of
the British Isles compared
to Antarctica

the South Pole

0°

Atlantic
Ocean

Prime Meridian

Southern Ocean

60°S

Indian
Ocean

Antarctic Circle

Queen Maud Land

60°E

Falkland
Islands

South
Orkney
Islands

60°W

Weddell Sea

ARGENTINA

South
Shetland
Islands

CHILE

Larsen
Ice Shelf

80°S

Antarctic Peninsula

Filchner
Ice Shelf

Ronne
Ice Shelf

Lambert Glacier

Mount
Menzies

Bellingshausen
Sea

Southern Ocean

Vinson Massif

South
Pole

Wilkes
Land

Ellsworth
Land

Mount Kirkpatrick

Pacific
Ocean

Marie-Byrd
Land

80°S

Ross
Ice Shelf

Mount Markham

120°W

Amundsen
Sea

Mount
Erebus

Ross Sea

120°E

Key

CHILE the names of countries are
shown in this type of lettering

country boundary

▲ peak or highest point

△ mountains

thick ice cap

sea covered by ice all year
sea covered by ice for part
of the year

⚑ scientists live here all year

Southern Ocean

180°

60°S

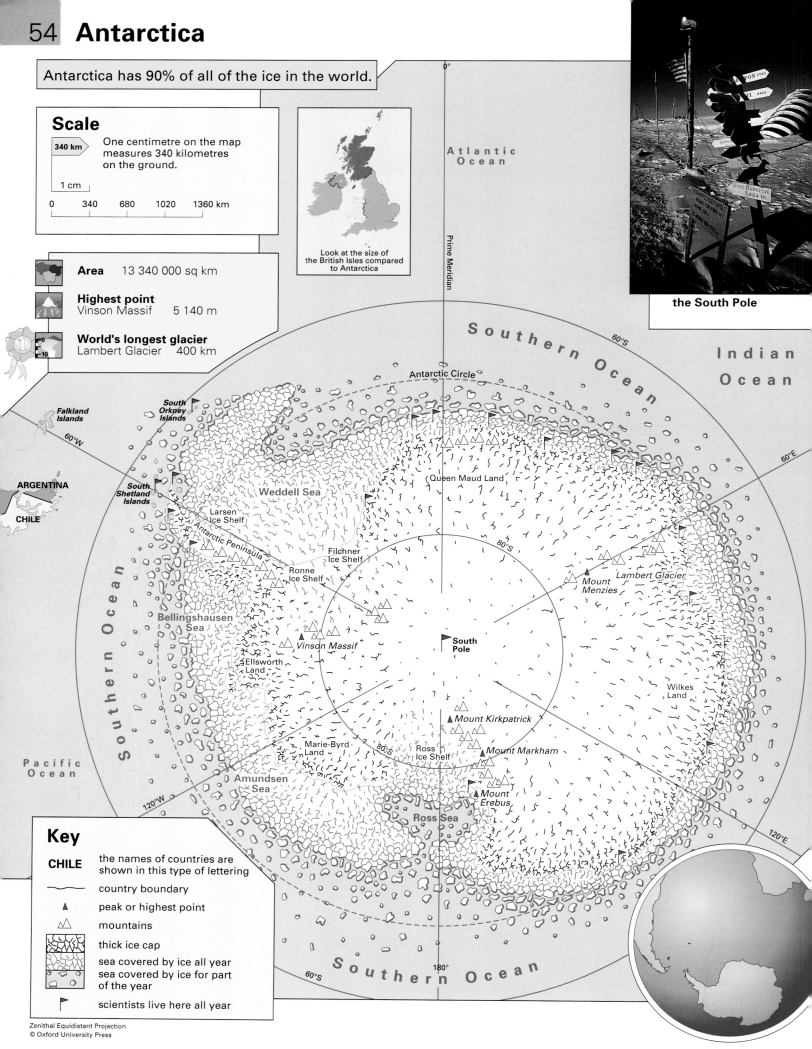

Most of the Arctic is a huge frozen ocean.

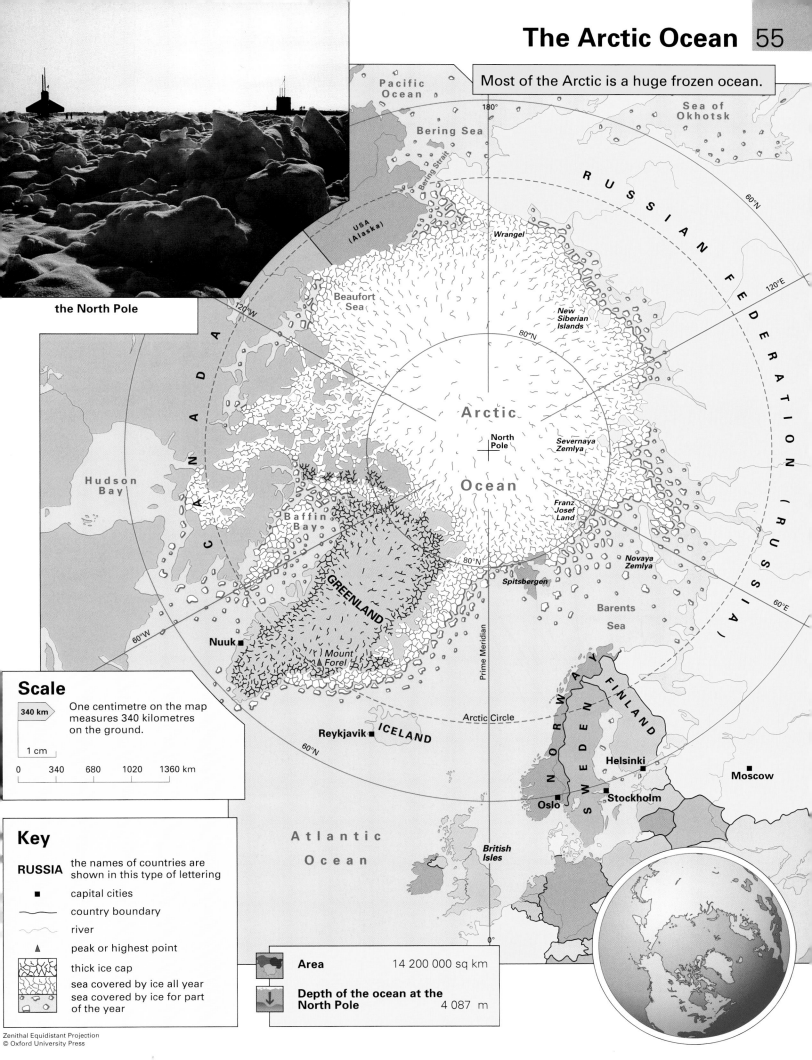

the North Pole

Pacific Ocean

Sea of Okhotsk

Bering Sea

180°

60°N

120°E

R U S S I A N   F E D E R A T I O N   (R U S S I A)

Wrangel

USA (Alaska)

Beaufort Sea

New Siberian Islands

80°N

120°W

Arctic

North Pole

Severnaya Zemlya

Ocean

Hudson Bay

C A N A D A

Franz Josef Land

Baffin Bay

Novaya Zemlya

80°N

Spitsbergen

60°E

GREENLAND

Barents Sea

60°W

Nuuk ■

Mount Forel

Prime Meridian

Arctic Circle

60°N

Reykjavik ■ **ICELAND**

N O R W A Y

F I N L A N D

Helsinki ■

Moscow ■

S W E D E N

Oslo ■ ■ Stockholm

Atlantic Ocean

British Isles

0°

Scale

▷ **340 km**

One centimetre on the map measures 340 kilometres on the ground.

1 cm

| 0 | 340 | 680 | 1020 | 1360 km |

Key

RUSSIA   the names of countries are shown in this type of lettering

■   capital cities

——   country boundary

～   river

▲   peak or highest point

▨   thick ice cap

⬚   sea covered by ice all year

⬚   sea covered by ice for part of the year

| | **Area** | 14 200 000 sq km |
| ↓ | **Depth of the ocean at the North Pole** | 4 087 m |

Two-thirds of the surface of the earth is covered with water. The rest is land.

Scale

One centimetre on the map measures 1050 kilometres on the ground at the Equator.

1050 km

1 cm

| 0 | 1050 | 2100 | 3150 | 4200 km |

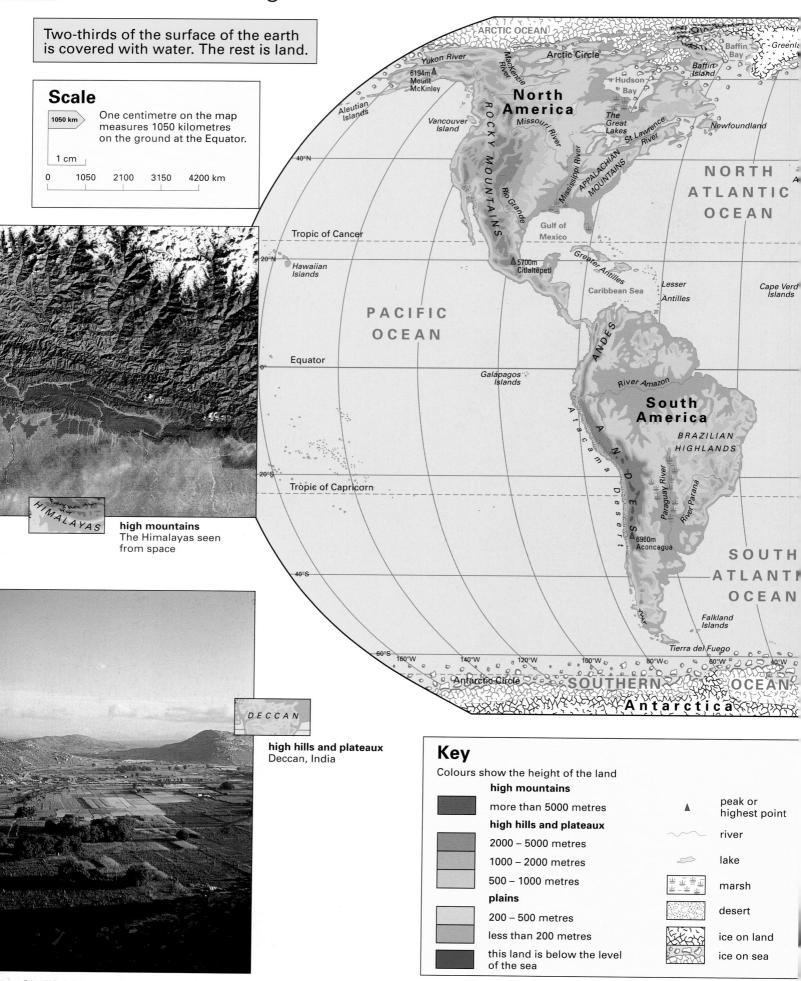

high mountains
The Himalayas seen from space

HIMALAYAS

DECCAN

high hills and plateaux
Deccan, India

Key

Colours show the height of the land

high mountains
more than 5000 metres

high hills and plateaux
2000 – 5000 metres
1000 – 2000 metres
500 – 1000 metres

plains
200 – 500 metres
less than 200 metres
this land is below the level of the sea

▲ peak or highest point
~ river
lake
marsh
desert
ice on land
ice on sea

Eckert IV Projection
© Oxford University Press

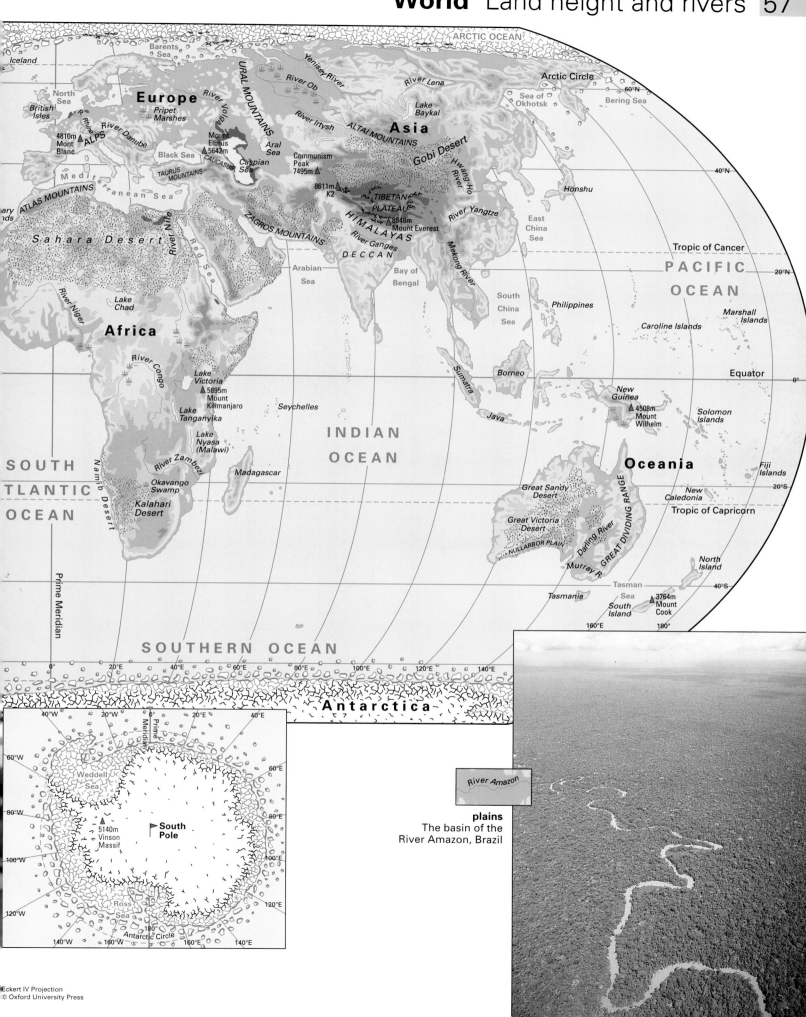

ARCTIC OCEAN

Iceland

Barents
Sea

North
Sea

British
Isles

Europe

Pripet
Marshes

R. Rhine
4810m Mont
Blanc ALPS

River Danube

River Volga

URAL MOUNTAINS

River Ob

Yenisey River

River Lena

Arctic Circle

60°N

Sea of
Okhotsk

Bering Sea

Mount
Elbrus
5642m
CAUCASUS

Black Sea

TAURUS
MOUNTAINS

Aral
Sea

Caspian
Sea

Communism
Peak
7495m

River Irtysh

ALTAI MOUNTAINS

Asia

Lake
Baykal

Gobi Desert

Hwang-Ho
River

Honshu

40°N

ATLAS MOUNTAINS

Mediterranean Sea

ZAGROS MOUNTAINS

8611m
K2

TIBETAN
PLATEAU

8848m
Mount Everest

HIMALAYAS

River Ganges

DECCAN

River Yangtze

Mekong River

East
China
Sea

Sahara Desert

River Nile

Red Sea

Arabian
Sea

Bay of
Bengal

South
China
Sea

Philippines

Tropic of Cancer

PACIFIC

OCEAN

20°N

River Niger

Lake
Chad

Africa

Caroline Islands

Marshall
Islands

River Congo

Lake
Victoria

5895m
Mount
Kilimanjaro

Seychelles

Sumatra

Borneo

Java

New
Guinea

4508m
Mount
Wilhelm

Solomon
Islands

Equator

0°

Lake
Tanganyika

Lake
Nyasa
(Malawi)

Madagascar

INDIAN

OCEAN

Oceania

Fiji
Islands

SOUTH

ATLANTIC

OCEAN

Namib Desert

River Zambezi

Okavango
Swamp

Kalahari
Desert

Great Sandy
Desert

Great Victoria
Desert

NULLARBOR PLAIN

Murray R.

Darling River

GREAT DIVIDING RANGE

New
Caledonia

Tropic of Capricorn

20°S

Prime Meridian

Tasman
Sea

Tasmania

South
Island

North
Island

3764m
Mount
Cook

40°S

160°E

180°

SOUTHERN OCEAN

0°

20°E

40°E

60°E

80°E

100°E

120°E

140°E

Antarctica

40°W

20°W

Prime
Meridian

20°E

40°E

60°W

60°E

80°W

Weddell
Sea

80°E

5140m
Vinson
Massif

South
Pole

100°W

100°E

120°W

Ross
Sea

120°E

140°W

180°

160°E

140°E

Antarctic Circle

River Amazon

plains
The basin of the
River Amazon, Brazil

Patterns of temperature and rainfall throughout the year make types of climate.

Scale

One centimetre on the map measures 1050 kilometres on the ground at the Equator.

1 cm

| 0 | 1050 | 2100 | 3150 | 4200 km |

Key

polar climate

continental climate

coastal climate

Mediterranean climate

desert climate

tropical climate

equatorial climate

high mountain climate

* places with record breaking climates

Hottest place
Al' Aziziyah (Libya)

Coldest place
Vostok (Antarctica)

Driest place
Arica, Atacama Desert (Chile)

Wettest place
Mawsynram (India)

Windiest place
Mount Washington (USA)

Snowiest place
Mount Rainier (USA)

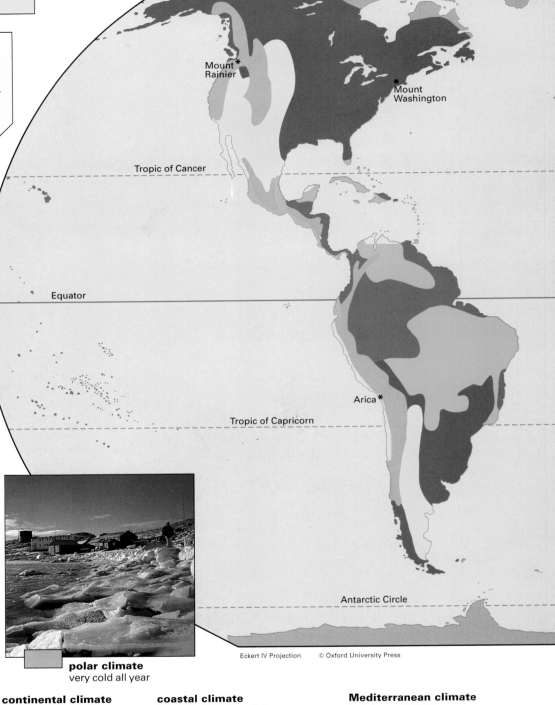

Arctic Circle

Mount Rainier *

Mount * Washington

Tropic of Cancer

Equator

Arica *

Tropic of Capricorn

Antarctic Circle

Eckert IV Projection   © Oxford University Press

polar climate
very cold all year

continental climate
very cold winters,
warmer summers

coastal climate
warm summers, mild winters,
rain all year

Mediterranean climate
hot dry summers,
warm wet winters

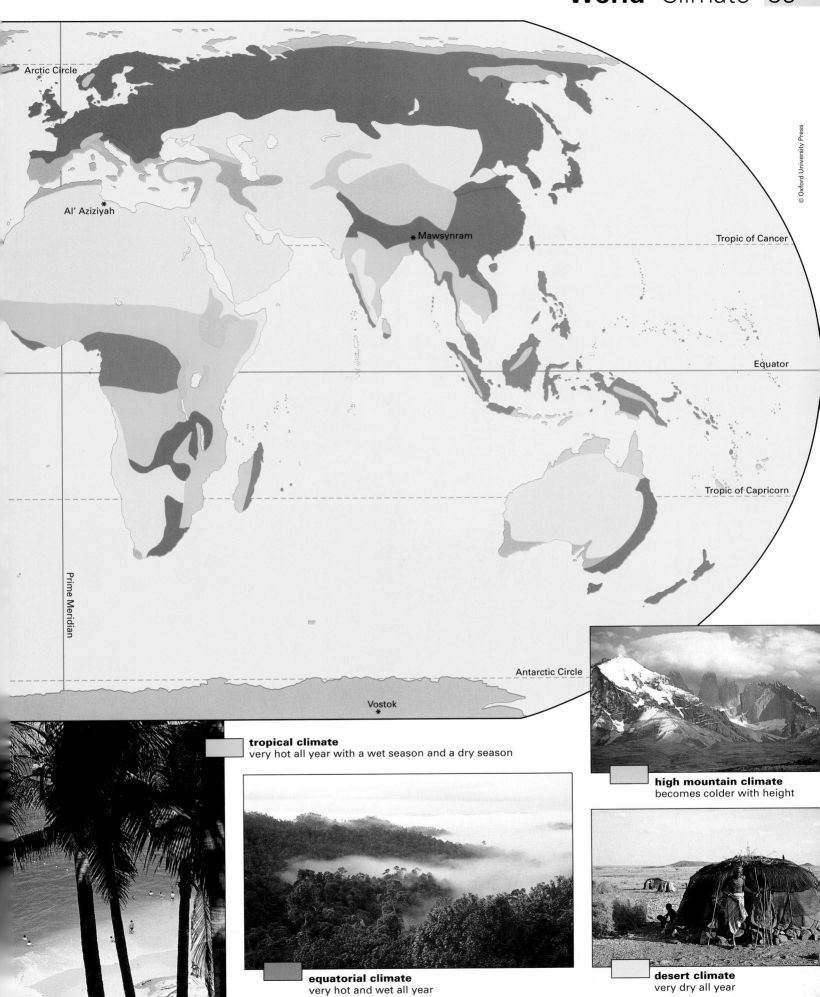

© Oxford University Press

Arctic Circle

Al' Aziziyah *

* Mawsynram

Tropic of Cancer

Equator

Tropic of Capricorn

Prime Meridian

Antarctic Circle

Vostok
*

tropical climate
very hot all year with a wet season and a dry season

high mountain climate
becomes colder with height

equatorial climate
very hot and wet all year

desert climate
very dry all year

Environments are our natural and human surroundings.

Scale

1050 km

One centimetre on the map measures 1050 kilometres on the ground at the Equator.

1 cm

| 0 | 1050 | 2100 | 3150 | 4200 km |

Key

⟋⟍	high mountains
🌲	cold forest
🌳	savannah
🌳	hot forest
	desert
	marsh
	ice on land
	ice on the sea
🏢	very large built up areas
∿	country boundary

Most natural environments have been influenced by people.

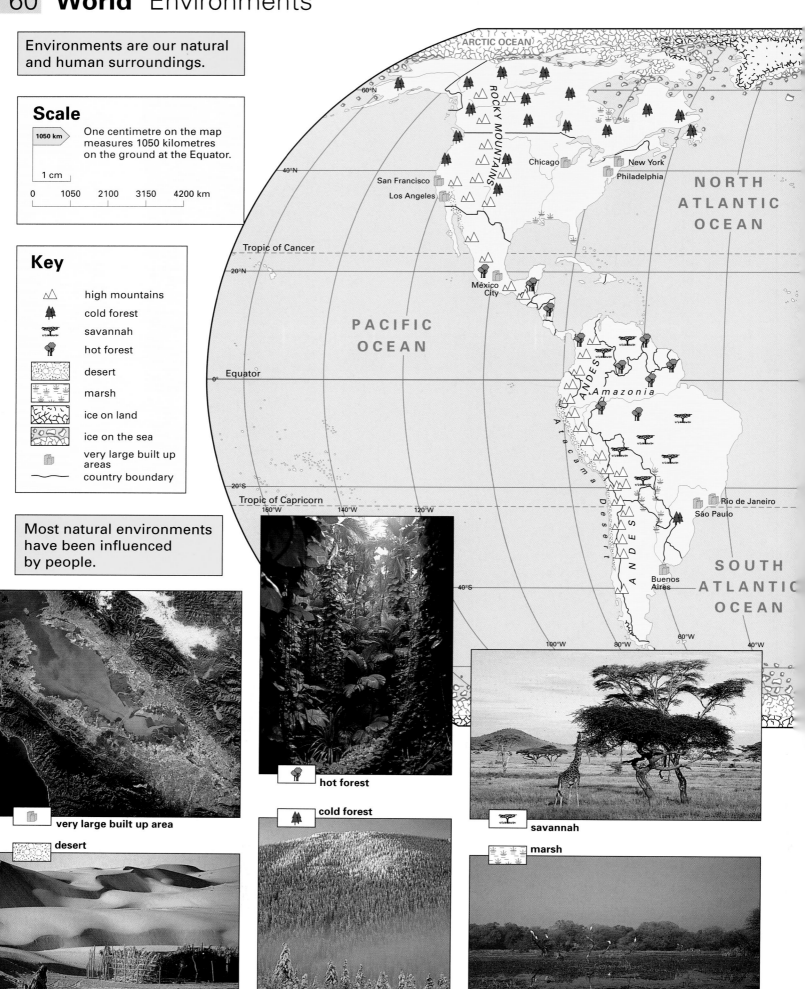

very large built up area

desert

hot forest

cold forest

savannah

marsh

ARCTIC OCEAN

60°N

ROCKY MOUNTAINS

Chicago

New York

San Francisco

Philadelphia

Los Angeles

NORTH ATLANTIC OCEAN

40°N

Tropic of Cancer

20°N

México City

PACIFIC OCEAN

Equator

0°

ANDES

Amazonia

Atacama Desert

20°S

Tropic of Capricorn

160°W   140°W   120°W

Rio de Janeiro

São Paulo

ANDES

SOUTH ATLANTIC OCEAN

Buenos Aires

40°S

100°W   80°W   60°W   40°W

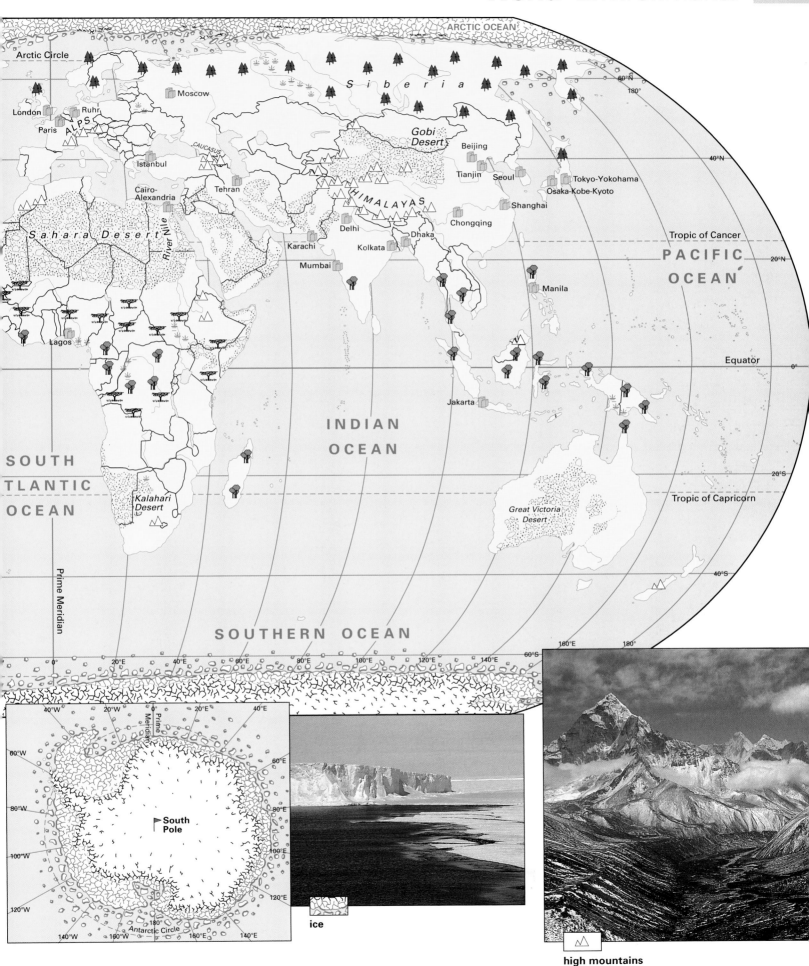

ARCTIC OCEAN

Arctic Circle

Siberia

Moscow

London
Ruhr
Paris ALPS
CAUCASUS
Istanbul

Gobi Desert

Beijing

60°N

180°

40°N

Tianjin
Seoul
Tokyo-Yokohama
Osaka-Kobe-Kyoto

Cairo-Alexandria
Tehran

HIMALAYAS

Sahara Desert

River Nile

Delhi

Shanghai
Chongqing

Karachi
Kolkata
Dhaka

Tropic of Cancer

PACIFIC
OCEAN

20°N

Mumbai

Manila

Equator 0°

Lagos

INDIAN
OCEAN

Jakarta

SOUTH
ATLANTIC
OCEAN

Kalahari Desert

Great Victoria Desert

20°S

Tropic of Capricorn

40°S

SOUTHERN OCEAN

160°E
180°

0° 20°E 40°E 60°E 80°E 100°E 120°E 140°E 60°E

40°W 20°W Prime Meridian 20°E 40°E

60°W
60°E

80°W
South Pole
80°E

100°W
100°E

120°W
120°E

140°W 160°W 180° 160°E 140°E
Antarctic Circle

ice

high mountains

People have damaged the natural environment in many parts of the world.

Scale

One centimetre on the map measures 1050 kilometres on the ground at the Equator.

1050 km

1 cm

0   1050   2100   3150   4200 km

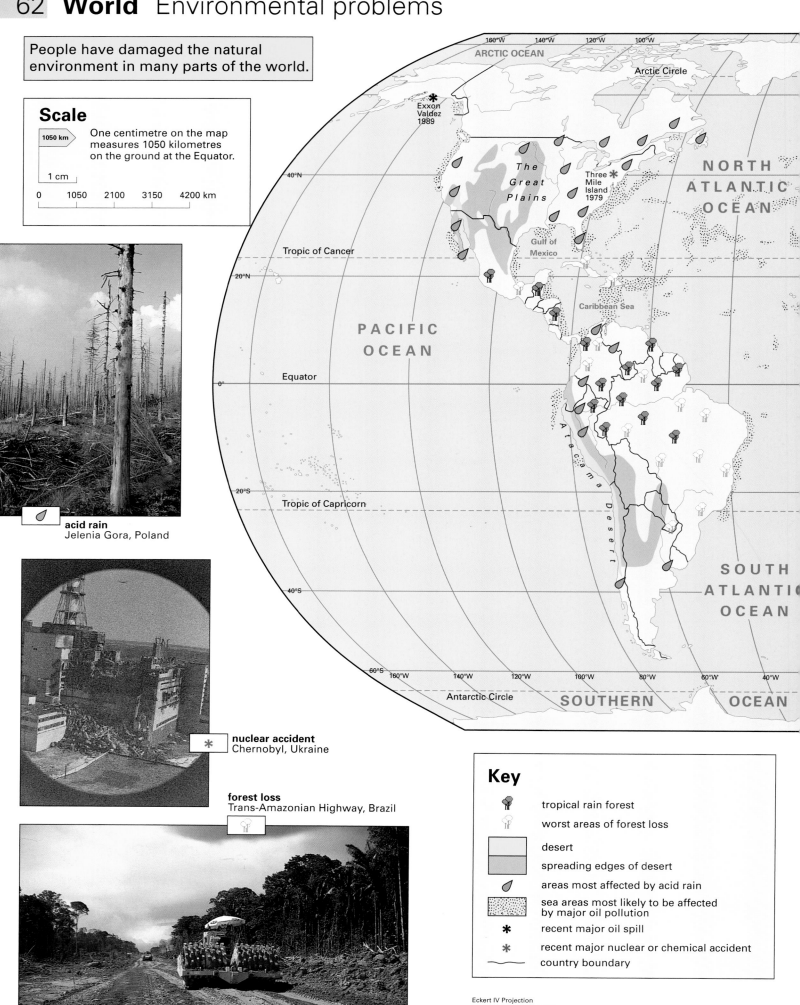

acid rain
Jelenia Gora, Poland

nuclear accident
Chernobyl, Ukraine

forest loss
Trans-Amazonian Highway, Brazil

ARCTIC OCEAN

Arctic Circle

Exxon Valdez 1989

The Great Plains

Three Mile Island 1979

NORTH ATLANTIC OCEAN

Tropic of Cancer

Gulf of Mexico

Caribbean Sea

PACIFIC OCEAN

Equator

Atacama Desert

Tropic of Capricorn

SOUTH ATLANTIC OCEAN

Antarctic Circle

SOUTHERN   OCEAN

Key

🌳 tropical rain forest

🌲 worst areas of forest loss

⬜ desert

🟫 spreading edges of desert

💧 areas most affected by acid rain

▨ sea areas most likely to be affected by major oil pollution

✳ recent major oil spill

✱ recent major nuclear or chemical accident

— country boundary

Eckert IV Projection
© Oxford University Press

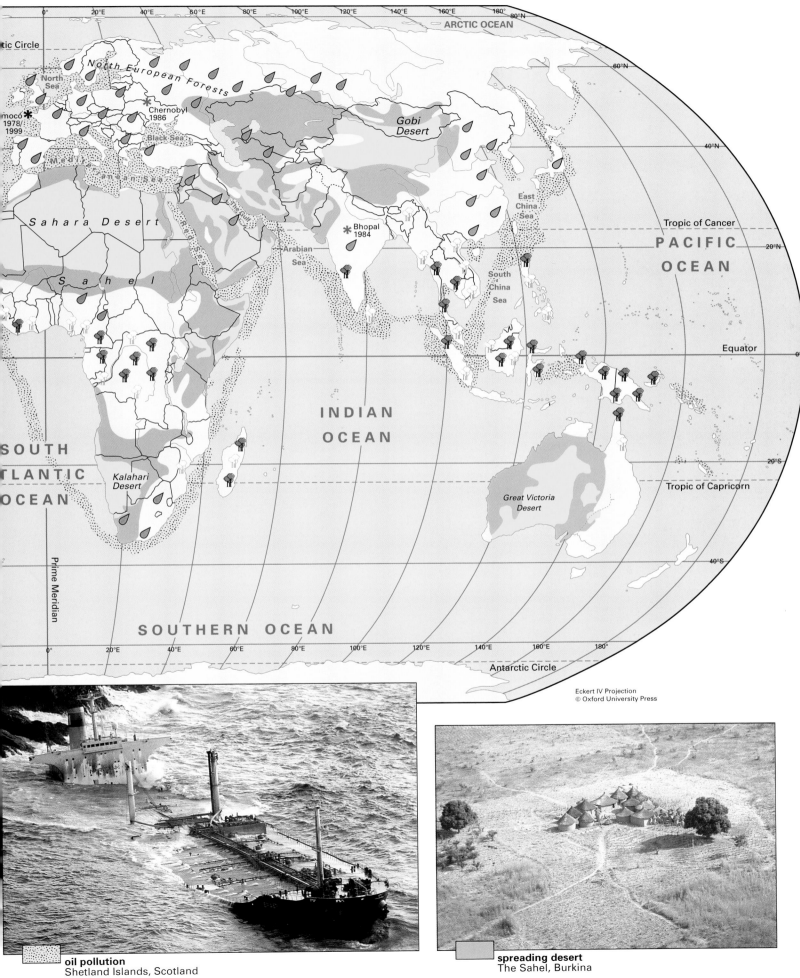

ARCTIC OCEAN

North European Forests

Gobi Desert

North Sea

moco 1978/ 1999

Chernobyl 1986

Black Sea

Mediterranean Sea

East China Sea

Sahara Desert

Tropic of Cancer

PACIFIC OCEAN

Sahel

The Gulf

Bhopal 1984

Red Sea

Arabian Sea

South China Sea

Equator

INDIAN OCEAN

SOUTH ATLANTIC OCEAN

Kalahari Desert

Tropic of Capricorn

Great Victoria Desert

Prime Meridian

SOUTHERN OCEAN

Antarctic Circle

Eckert IV Projection
© Oxford University Press

oil pollution
Shetland Islands, Scotland

spreading desert
The Sahel, Burkina

Some parts of the world are crowded, others have very few people.

Scale

One centimetre on the map measures 1050 kilometres on the ground at the equator.

1050 km

1 cm

0 1050 2100 3150 4200 km

Key

one million (1 000 000) people live near each dot

very many people

many people

few people

the world's largest cities – each has more than 6 million people

Welfare

Some people in the world are rich. Many people are poor, or hungry, or suffering as a result of war.

rich countries — This colour shows the 25 richest countries in the world. Not everyone in these countries is rich but most live comfortably.

poor countries — This colour shows the 40 poorest countries in the world. Not everyone in these countries is poor but most are in need.

war — This symbol shows places where there has recently been a war.

famine — This symbol shows places where there has recently been a shortage of food.

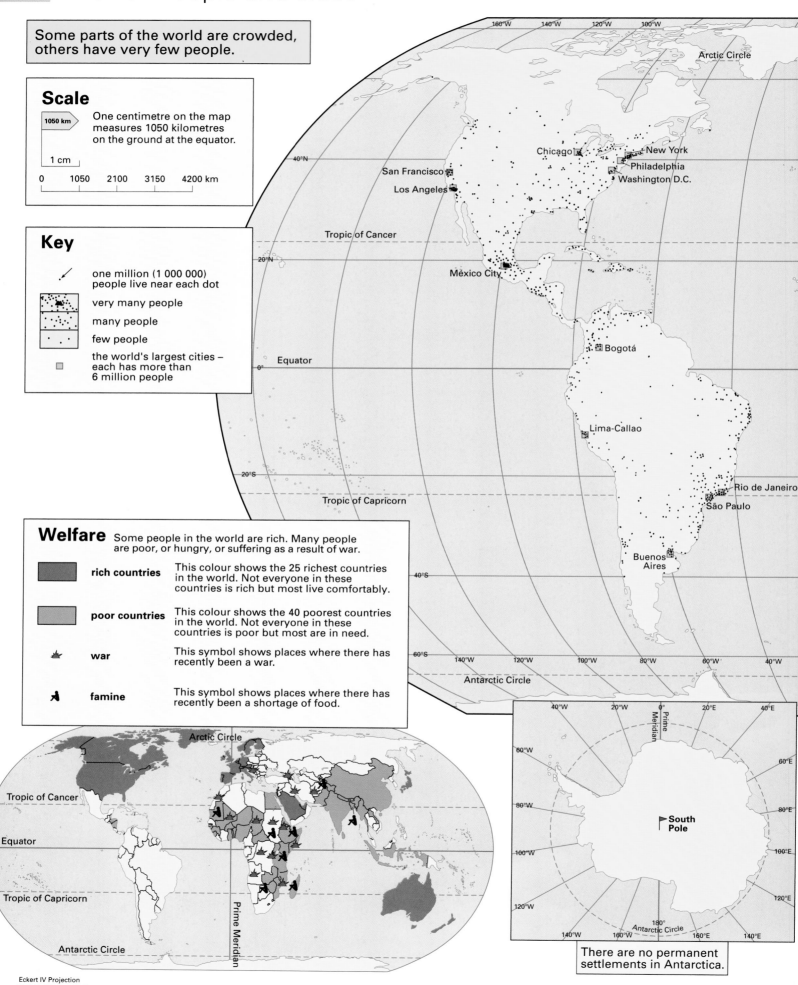

Arctic Circle

Chicago New York Philadelphia Washington D.C.

San Francisco Los Angeles

México City

Tropic of Cancer

Bogotá

Equator

Lima-Callao

Tropic of Capricorn

Rio de Janeiro

São Paulo

Buenos Aires

Antarctic Circle

Arctic Circle
Tropic of Cancer
Equator
Tropic of Capricorn
Antarctic Circle
Prime Meridian

South Pole

There are no permanent settlements in Antarctica.

Eckert IV Projection
© Oxford University Press

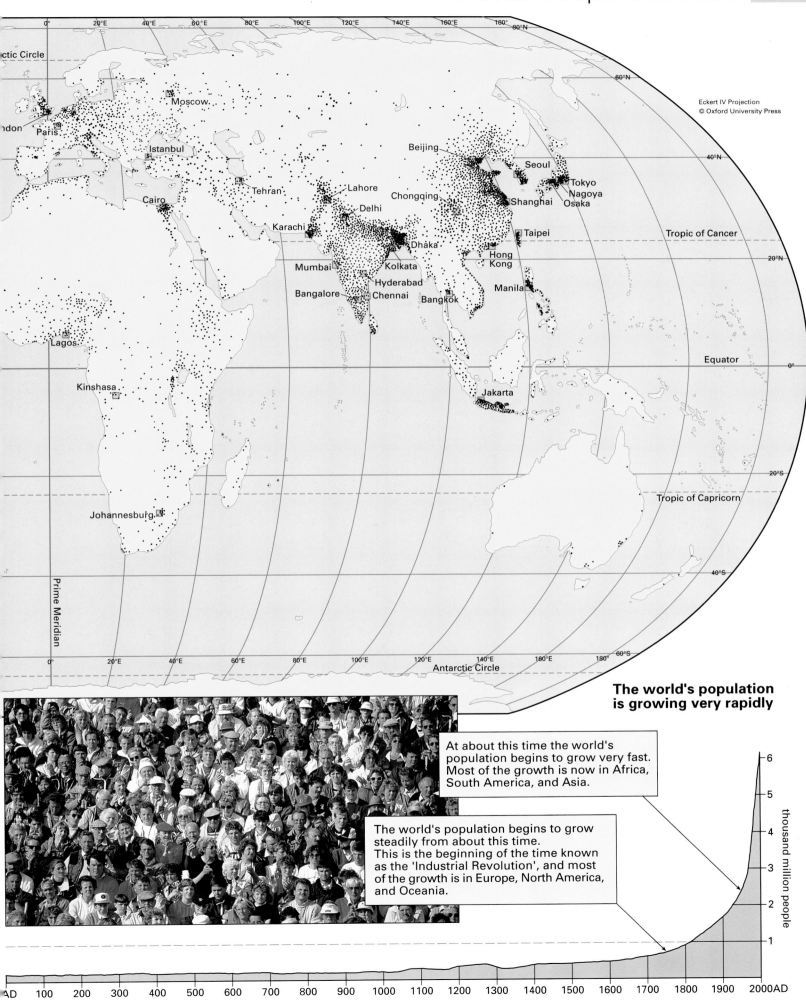

Eckert IV Projection
© Oxford University Press

Arctic Circle

London
Paris
Moscow
Istanbul
Tehran
Cairo
Lahore
Karachi
Delhi
Mumbai
Bangalore
Hyderabad
Chennai
Kolkata
Dhaka
Beijing
Chongqing
Shanghai
Seoul
Tokyo
Nagoya
Osaka
Taipei
Hong Kong
Bangkok
Manila
Jakarta
Lagos
Kinshasa
Johannesburg

Tropic of Cancer
Equator
Tropic of Capricorn

Prime Meridian
Antarctic Circle

The world's population is growing very rapidly

At about this time the world's population begins to grow very fast. Most of the growth is now in Africa, South America, and Asia.

The world's population begins to grow steadily from about this time. This is the beginning of the time known as the 'Industrial Revolution', and most of the growth is in Europe, North America, and Oceania.

thousand million people

6
5
4
3
2
1

AD 100 200 300 400 500 600 700 800 900 1000 1100 1200 1300 1400 1500 1600 1700 1800 1900 2000AD

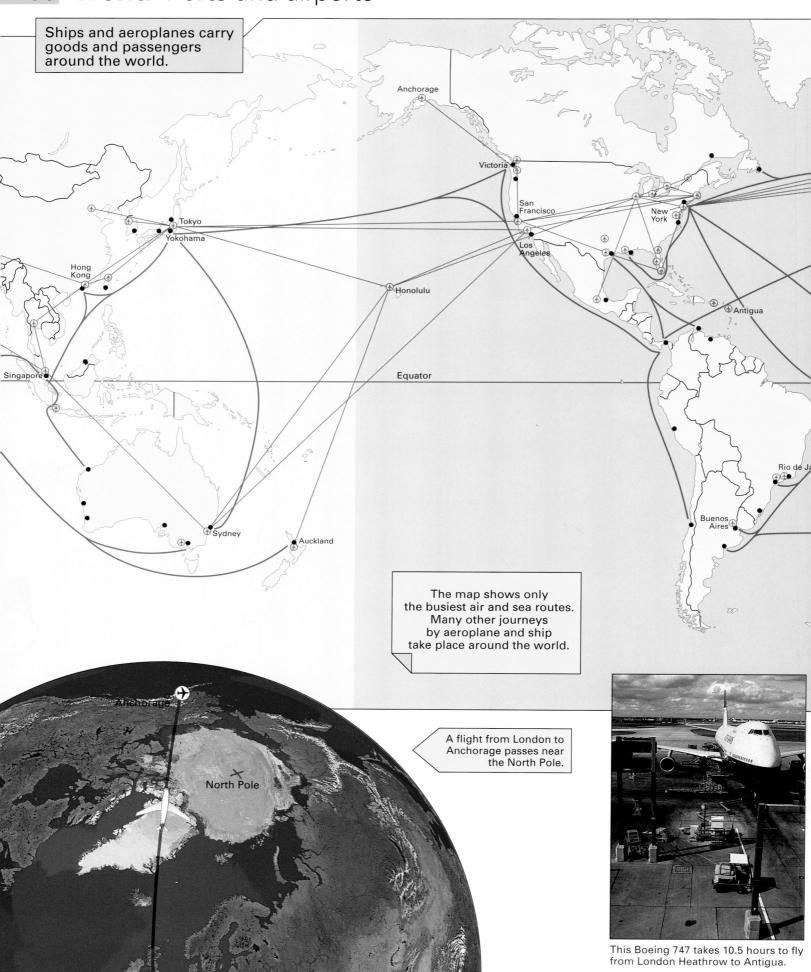

Ships and aeroplanes carry
goods and passengers
around the world.

Anchorage

Victoria

San
Francisco

New
York

Tokyo

Yokohama

Los
Angeles

Hong
Kong

Honolulu

Antigua

Singapore

Equator

Rio de Ja

Buenos
Aires

Sydney

Auckland

The map shows only
the busiest air and sea routes.
Many other journeys
by aeroplane and ship
take place around the world.

Anchorage

North Pole

A flight from London to
Anchorage passes near
the North Pole.

London

This Boeing 747 takes 10.5 hours to fly
from London Heathrow to Antigua.

Gall Projection
© Oxford University Press

Moscow

Hamburg

London

Kuwait

Mumbai

Lagos

Hong Kong

Singapore

Tokyo

Yokohama

Honolulu

Equator

Sydney

Auckland

This oil tanker takes 18 days to sail from Kuwait to the United Kingdom.

...container ship takes 25 days to sail ...m Hamburg to Buenos Aires.

Scale

1200 km

One centimetre on the map measures 1200 kilometres on the ground at the Equator.

1 cm

| 0 | 1200 | 2400 | 3600 | 4800 km |

It is about 40 000 kilometres (25 000 miles) around the world.

Key

	international boundary
	main shipping lanes
•	major port
	main air routes
⊕	major airport

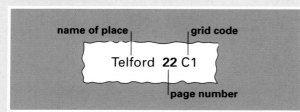

name of place   grid code

Telford **22** C1

page number